Go **Happy** Yourself!!

HOW REINVENTING THE WHEEL OF YOUR LIFE
CAN MAKE YOUR JOY BLOSSOM!

Jamie Lee Carmichael

Printed in the United States of America

ISBN-13:978-1976579738
ISBN-10:1976579732

First Printing, 2017

Jamie Lee Carmichael
www.gohappyyourself.com

Cover Design by Ahsan Chuhadry

CONTENTS

ACKNOWLEDGEMENTS

I have dreamed of writing a book since I was in the fourth grade. I thank all my English and Creative Writing teachers since then for instilling in me the love to write. Way too many to name here, but especially Leila Semah (4th grade, P.S. 181) and James Mangano (Sheepshead Bay High School.)

I chose this topic to write about first because happiness is the ultimate goal that everyone seeks, but that always seems to elude us. I don't think a day goes by that it doesn't come up in conversations with friends, family and clients. So for all of those folks that make happiness a priority in their lives and the ones that need to – thank you.

Thank you Clare for my graceful book interior and Ahsan for my beautiful cover design.

Thank you Angie Gwinn for the cover photographs. An accomplished vocal artist, you may have missed another calling as a stupendous photographer!

My sister, Lynne, my first best friend. I love all our shared memories…we have some funny ones…(here – hold this!) I love how you can love me and beat me over the head at the same time – when I need it of course!

My sisters from another mother – technically my cousins, but they adopted me as one of their own. Their love and belief in me is unending – Sharon, Mary and especially Judy, Dona and Monica (Nina).

Every once in awhile, God will grant you a true, true best friend, and in September of 1968, God brought Donna into my life. Donna and I have been best friends since we were 10 years old. There have been years when we've been separated and lost touch, but during those times, we both still referred to each other as our best friend. When we get together it's like no time has passed at all.

I don't live near any of these wonderful women in my life, but I know I couldn't live without any of them!

To Boo Boo Kitty Face and Chicken McNugget…I love you as much today as I did the moment you came into the world. Though our paths today move in different directions, my love for you is constant and moves with you wherever your life takes you. I wish you love, happiness and success in everything you do.

There are so many other incredible people in my life that I have met along the way and that have either changed and/or enriched it. They are (in no particular order) Bill Reschke, Rick Caswell, Jay and Janine Malave (and Cody!), Chris Peet, Debbi, Selena, Sue and June Bug. Lynda, Wendy and the rest of the Calendar Girls. Glen. Cindy, Linda and Sharon. Amber and Joe. Grace, Mary and Kathleen. Beckie, Regina and the other Fight Club for Women members. Aunt Sheila, Mags and Ted, My cousins Jill, Ellie and Mary Lou. My life is immeasurably better because of you.

Finally a shout out to my friend and fellow coach Noelle Landis who, aside from being a great friend and confidant, introduced me to my coach and mentor, Rick Gabrielly. Rick kicked my butt to get this book written. I experienced some tough love writing under extreme personal pressure, but Rick refused to give up on me. I can say without hesitation that this book would not have been possible without Rick Gabrielly.

Thank you all – I love you!

This book is dedicated to sisters…the ones born to you,
and the ones you find along the way.
We can never, ever have too many.

FOREWORD

Jamie Lee Carmichael wears many hats. She's a native-New Yorker, who's spent as much time helping others in her work and personal life as she has working on herself.

She's bright, both intellectually as well as personally, she's realistic, and she knows when to take a good risk. Jamie is a joyful giver. With her strong values, she has built a foundation on integrity, perseverance and family, and takes pride in her career, loved ones and transformation. As the creator of the brand "Go Happy Yourself," Jamie is embarking on her most exciting journey yet. And it's all for You.

And now, she's an author.

What is "Go Happy Yourself?" It's more than a brand and book title. It's a mindset. It's a life design plan. It's a mantra that feeds the longing in each of us. We all want to be happy.

And what is Happiness? And why is it so hard to find?

If you study human history, we've become more complex with each passing year. Why does it feel like the good life and finding your happy seems further away than ever?

Today, we've made life much more complicated. Why do we do this?

Simple. We get lost in the things outside of us. Things we can't control. The people, events and thoughts that live beyond our self.

In this transformational book, Jamie Lee gives us a clear roadmap to finding our own "Happy." A simple, yet powerful process that anyone can master.

And she learned from her own journey. A journey of trial and error. A fearless trek across the heart, going where she needed to with clarity and purpose. Sticking to her values of truth and hard work, no matter what her past stories said. Jamie drove forward. And now You can win because of her inner and outer work.

So now you can "Go Happy Yourself" too.

If you've ever wanted to be truly happy, now you have an owner's manual. Let this joyologist take you on the ride of a lifetime. Jamie knows Happy. C'mon, jump in with her. You'll be "happy" you did.

Rick Gabrielly

Author, Life Designer and Global Wellness Entrepreneur

August 2017, New York

INTRODUCTION

Most folks are as happy as they make their minds up to be.
Abraham Lincoln

If I had to pick one thing that I hear from my new coaching clients day in and day out – when asked what they want from their lives – is that they "just want to be happy." When I probe them for what that means, it's usually a mix of answers – they believe more money, a better relationship, losing weight, a bigger house – will make them happy. They pursue happiness with a vengeance, when in fact it could be the very pursuit of their happiness that keeps them unhappy. It's like they are driving down a road looking for the sign that says: "You are now entering Happiness – Population: – a lot less than you think."

We're always chasing that one thing that will make us happy…as soon as I lose 50 pounds I'll be happy. If I could just land that promotion, boy would I be happy. If she says she'll marry me – that will make me happy. Happiness is always just at the other end of the rainbow…except that we never seem to get there – even when we do. Losing 50 pounds will make you feel better and probably look better, but in the long run the weight loss doesn't make you happy. Doubling your salary makes it easier to pay the bills and do fun things, but the money can't BUY you happiness. I know, right? It just doesn't seem fair, does it? But there is good news – you already have everything you need to live a happier life. Everything you need is already inside of you and it won't cost you one darn penny!

Case in point from my own life. From the time I was a kid, all I wanted was to be in a relationship. I've had several, but they were all wrong. I have been single for a long while now, and no matter how much good was in my life, there was always this shadow hanging over me…"I just want a boyfriend. If I had a boyfriend I would be happy." I've said it to myself, I've prayed for it, I've told everyone who I ever spent 5 minutes with. Finally, about a year ago, after sessions and sessions with my own coach, she finally lost it and said to me, "Jamie, if you want a boyfriend, go out and get one for God's sake!" She said, "If you wanted a job, it wouldn't take you five years to find one, why is it taking you five years to find a boyfriend? If that's what you want, go out and get it. Approach it the way you would if you were looking for a job."

So, I did just that. I immediately got on Match.com. Put my picture and profile out there. This was a huge step for me, because I am not a fan of online dating. But, I had a goal and I was determined. I got quite a few responses, winks and communications. I started conversations with a couple of guys and two even progressed to phone calls. One of those guys seemed really interested and we had a lot in common, but as we continued to talk, the strangest thing happened. I realized that I really didn't want to meet him. I didn't want a boyfriend. I didn't want a relationship. It had nothing to do with him, it was all me. What I thought I wanted for so many years was finally within my grasp, and I realized I didn't want it after all.

Because of my circumstances, I am the primary caregiver to my 92 year old father, my time is very precious. A new relationship takes time and effort and focus on the other person. I didn't feel I had the time, and even if I could find it, I didn't want to spend it on someone else. If I was going to have extra time, I was going to spend it on myself!

Can I tell you what that realization did to my happiness level? It EXPLODED it! I was deliriously happy with the fact that I DON'T WANT A BOYFRIEND! It was as if I had just been let out of prison after all these years. All these years searching, wishing, hoping and praying for something that never materialized. It played havoc with my confidence and self-worth. Why couldn't I find love? Was I unworthy? Why does everyone else have someone and I'm alone? Now, I know that it is my choice. At least for now, I am focusing on my caregiving duties and my own personal endeavors. Now, I'm free to do the things I have to do and pursue the things I want to pursue – on my own terms, on my own timeline…If someone should happen to come along and the time is right – so be it, but until then, I am complete all by myself.

So you can achieve happiness, but you can't pursue it. In fact, if we could rewrite the Constitution, I think it should say "You have the right to CHOOSE happiness" because, when it comes down to it – happiness is a choice.

Researchers have found that happiness is determined by three different factors. Circumstance, genetics and then by our thoughts and actions. But here's the kicker. Circumstance only influences about 10% of our happiness. 50% is influenced by genetics, (so yes, there really are glass half full and glass half empty people) and 40% by our thoughts and actions.

That's HUGE! While we can't do much about genetics and it often feels like we don't have a lot of control about our circumstances, there is a lot you can do when it comes to how you think and what you do. In other words, science proves that you have control over a big chunk of your own personal happiness.

For example, which do you consider yourself - a glass half full or a half empty person? This is a great way to illustrate that there are often two sides to any story and you have a choice is how you view things. And that choice in turn determines how happy you feel. Happiness then becomes a choice you make every single day.

You can choose to see the glass as half empty, focus on the fact that you're almost done drinking that nice glass of iced tea. With that attitude, you're more likely to feel a little depressed about your tea. If, on the other hand, you focus on the fact that the glass is still half full and you still have plenty of yummy, iced cold tea to sip on, your mood improves and you're increasing your happiness.

When you look at it that way, happiness is really a conscious choice you make, or more accurately, it's the result of many choices you make during your day. You decide which changes you are going to make to your life – like eating better – being grateful and some other things we'll talk about in this book that will help you increase how happy you feel at any given moment.

We can't control some of the situations that pop into our lives, we can control the decisions we make and the attitude we show to the world in reacting to those situations. You may or may not have a naturally sunny disposition, but you can make a choice each day to be happier – and that is huge.

Last but not least, it's important to remember that we can't be 100% happy all the time. And that's a good thing. Life would get boring and it's the darkest of times that make the good times shine all the brighter. During those dark times it helps to remember that no matter how hard and tough and maybe even desperate things seem right now, they won't be able to influence your emotions and your mood for much longer. Brighter days are ahead of you and you will find a way to reclaim your happiness and joy.

When you decide to choose happiness, you're making a commitment – a total commitment. That means setting a goal to be happy and dedicating yourself to do what it takes to reach that goal. We commit to a relationship when we get married, we commit to a job or a career, and we may be committed to a hobby. It's not always easy, but we usually stick with it.

Now that we're committed, it's just a matter of daily practice until the new behavior or action has become a true habit. A habit, by the way, is something you do without conscious thought or effort – like brushing your teeth every morning. Before we can cultivate these habits, we have to know what truly makes us happy.

The rest of this book is designed to help you figure that out. So, if you'll join me, we'll find out why your happiness matters, and then we'll discover what your "Wheel of Happiness" looks like – which comprises eight key areas of life – your physical environment, friends & family, love, fun & recreation, your health, your spirituality & personal growth, career and money. I'll wrap it up with some discussion on habits, and then provide you with a journal to help get you started in cultivating your habits so that you can…

Go Happy Yourself!!

CHAPTER ONE

Why Your **Happiness** Matters

Between the stress in our personal lives and the chaotic world around us, it is easy to get sucked into a feeling of doom and gloom. If you tune into the news even for just a little while, it seems that not a day goes by without some sort of disaster or tragedy striking. Add to that the usual political climate and it's no wonder that we feel like there isn't a whole lot to smile about these days.

Yet, at the same time how happy we are and feel makes a huge difference in all areas of our own lives and how we affect the lives of others. When you're in a good mood, you're more motivated to get stuff done. This, of course, means that your productivity will go up and work seems effortless. You also tend to do better work when you're happily invested in what you do. I'm sure you noticed both of these in your own life. If you're in a job or doing something that you love, time flies, work flies off your desk, and you're happily motivated to do a great job. If you're unhappy on the other hand, the hours drag, you're only half-heartedly in it, and as a result, work takes longer, and if you're honest, the quality isn't as high as you could make it. Are you trolling Facebook as you pretend to work? Yep, I thought so! You're putting in the hours, but you can't wait to head back home.

Of course, work isn't the only place happiness affects both your productivity and the quality of your "work." When you're happy, it's easier to get through the chores at home, get the shopping done, and cook a healthy meal for the family. Best of all is that happiness is contagious. By being yourself, you're affecting the mood of everyone around you in a positive way. This in turn will help you stay happier. It's a positively reinforced happiness loop.

Being in a good mood makes you a much more patient person. This is important to help with all relationships in your life. You know you are a much better parent, caregiver, spouse, or co-worker when you're patient. When you're stressed out and unhappy, it's easy to snap at someone and hurt their feelings without really meaning to do so. You're better at explaining, sharing and a better listener when you're patient and content.

Your happiness even affects your health. Happy people are less likely to get sick. It seems that smiles boost your immune system (who knew?!) A good mood will even help you heal faster and recover quicker from an illness. It's amazing how much happiness can affect your physical health in a positive way. Happiness, and laughing, in particular is a great stress buster. Just that act alone can reverse all the negative effects that stress can have on your body and mind.

So, in other words, happiness is important because it can have a positive effect on your mind, body and others around you. The good news is that you don't have to wait for happy times to appear. You have a lot of control over how you feel and how happy you are…in fact, you have all of the control. I cannot stress this enough – it is that important: Happiness is a choice we make day by day, hour by hour, and situation by situation. Isn't it time you took control and CHOSE happiness?

How you feel matters and it has a direct impact on your life and that of your loved ones or those that you spend a lot of time with. That is why it is so important to take the time to work on happiness. Of course, it should all start with you. As in an airplane you're told that in case of an emergency, you have to put your oxygen mask on first before helping others…you have to first be in a place of happiness before you can make anyone else happy…so let's spend a few minutes trying to focus on you.

It seems that happiness goes hand in hand with self-confidence, accepting your circumstances and living in the now. This is an important realization you need to have to increase your happiness. It's not about having everything you've ever wanted and everything being perfect. It's about living in the moment and being grateful for what you do have.

Because of this, as you work on being happier you'll start to notice that you feel better about yourself. It is also a fact that when you're happy, you're more productive. When you're more productive, you feel like you're making progress and feel pride in what you're accomplishing, which in turn increases your confidence – which then bumps up your happiness factor. The end result is that you get a lot more done than when you're feeling mopey. Happiness is a great energy booster.

Of course, this is by no means an extensive list. We each have our own individual reasons why we want to increase our happiness outside of the obvious – we want to be happier. Find your own internal motivation. Maybe you want to be happier so that you are a better spouse, parent, friend, sibling or child…

Are you beginning to see that you can increase your own happiness? When some folks find their happiness they feel it's their mission to make others happy. It's a great thought, but I just have to say here that there is nothing, and I mean nothing you can do to MAKE another person happy. Happiness comes from within, and just like you, they will have to find it for themselves, but working towards your own happiness is not only great for yourself and your own life, but your mood and how you feel about yourself and your circumstances can have a profound impact on the people and world around you.

I have seen this play out recently in my own life. Caregiving is very stressful work…especially when you're doing it alone. I've been feeling the burden, and I had been letting it take me down. It was reflected in every part of my life. I became short or snapped at my Dad – when he did nothing to provoke it. I was sullen and pessimistic. I stopped finding joy in the big things – let alone the little things. I stopped accepting invitations from my friends, and then they eventually stopped extending them. Who wants to be around that kind of attitude?

So see – even a person whose business it is to be happy struggles with it sometimes! However, when I noticed what was happening, I stopped and thought about it. Did I really want to feel this way? Of course not. I made the decision – I CHOSE to be happier. Then, when I made the switch, it was like the shades were pulled up. People around me became happier – and there were more people around me! When you're anxious and stressed out, people tend to steer clear of you. When you're happy and content on the other hand, people tend to gravitate to you. You become kinder and a lot more patient. Kindness and patience are so important in dealing and interacting with other people and makes a huge difference in how they feel about themselves.

Being patient and kind make you a much better parent. Kids are still learning and they will do stupid stuff along the way. They also have a lot of questions and learn through repetition. Being supportive and understanding can take a lot of patience when you're dealing with little ones. Being a patient and kind parent will go a long way towards raising happy and well-adjusted kids.

I'm at the other end of the spectrum, caring for my father. A 92 year old man, dealing with his own mortality. He needs kindness and compassion at this stage. Being happy makes me a better daughter and caregiver. It is not easy, but it's a choice that I make – sometimes 100 times a day – and to be quite honest, he deserves it. When I am happier and project that to

4

my Dad, he in turn is happier as well. Although it's hard work, I don't want him to spend his last days/weeks/months feeling like he is a burden... no one should go out like that.

The same holds true with our romantic relationships. Being a happy person helps you relax, appreciate your partner and as a result make you more likely to see his or her point of view. Overall it will be more fun to hang out and spend time together in a fun and positive way, which will deepen and improve your relationship further. Being happy will make you a happier spouse, or significant other and thus improve your marriage/relationship.

Last but not least, being a happier person makes you a better friend, acquaintance and co-worker. By working on your own happiness, you're improving the lives of those around you and your relationship with them, no matter what that might be.

As you work on your own happiness and on improving your relationships, something else interesting happens. You start to notice that those around you – even strangers - are in a better mood as well. Give it a try. Go head out on some errands and put a big smile on your face. Make an effort to have a happy interaction with people around you and you'll notice that they can't help but smile back. That's because happiness is infectious and contagious. I'm sure you've experienced this yourself. You can't help but smile when you're around a young child that's smiling, laughing and giggling.

By working on your own level of happiness and being willing to show it with a pretty smile, you're also spreading that same happiness to those around you. Here is where things get interesting. As you improve the mood of those around you, it in turn bounces back to you, increasing your own levels of happiness and joy. By making a conscious effort to be happier, you are creating a self-propelling cycle of positivity that will come back around to help you. That's a pretty neat concept, and one that we are very much in need of today.

Of course all this self-perpetuating happiness won't go unnoticed. Just like the butterfly wing can create small changes in air currents that ripple and turn into a hurricane (the butterfly effect), your small acts of kindness that are a result of your own increased happiness can have huge effects on the world.

If we all worked on becoming happier, kinder, more patient, more tolerant and more productive people, just think of how much better this world we live in would become. We could avoid armed conflicts, redistribute resources more equally and make sure everyone has a safe place to live and food in their bellies.

While that's a beautiful concept, I realize that it may also be a bit of a pipe dream. But does that mean that we should stop spreading happiness and joy? Of course not. Even, and especially the small things matter. Think back on the times when you were down on your luck or having a particularly rough day. Did that smile or kind word from a friend or stranger make a difference in your life? I'm sure it did.

Just this weekend, I took my Dad out for ice cream. He need to buy some birthday cards, so I had to get him out of the car and into the store. When we got back to the car – he got in and I was putting his walker into the trunk. This is something I've done hundreds of times, and it doesn't get any easier. Things fall out of his little pouch, the wires catch on something, the wheels get stuck, and it barely fits in the trunk. So there I was struggling as usual when a man walking through the parking lot on his own way to run his own errand, stopped and asked me if I needed assistance. I thanked him but declined, as I had just gotten the thing in the trunk, but it really brightened my day. That one little act of kindness.

Work on your happiness, spread the joy and do your part to use this new-found "superpower" to start making the world a better place, one smile and one kind word or act at a time.

CHAPTER TWO

Wheel of **Happiness**

How satisfied we are with our own lives has a direct impact on our happiness. For that reason, the first exercise I give my coaching clients is to complete the "Wheel of Happiness." When I was obtaining my coaching certification this tool was provided to the students. At first glance, I thought it was kind of lame and thought, "I'm never going to use this with my clients," but as I began coaching real people, what became overwhelmingly obvious to me is that people don't really have a clear picture in their heads of what would actually bring them real happiness. They're so busy in their day-to-day lives that they don't even have time to consider it, and it's usually not until some crisis or life-changing event occurs that they even think about it. This exercise will give you an opportunity to focus on eight key areas of life and give you a chance to assess how happy you are in each area and which areas need work. I've prettied up the wheel a bit and turned it into a flower, but you'll get the idea when you look at it on the following page. You can also download a copy of the wheel by going to this page on my website: www.gohappyyourself.com/bloom

Take a few minutes or as long as you'd like to really contemplate each area. I'll meet you on the other side.

1. **Physical Environment:** Take a look around you where you spend most of your time. In your home. In your bedroom. At work at your desk. In your city. Your hometown. When you look around your physical environment how does it make you feel? Give it a number between 1 to 10, where one is I just can't stand this place another second, to 10 which would be like there is no other place I'd rather be. When you have your number, look at the corresponding wedge on the bloom of happiness and imagine where that number would be in that wedge…For instance, if you rated your space a 5, you would be about halfway up the pie shaped wedge from the center. Go ahead and put a line straight across the wedge and with you pen, pencil or marker color the wedge in from the center.

2. **Family and Friends:** So this section pertains to your family - all family with the exception of your spouse or significant other. How satisfied are you with the relationships you have with your parents and siblings, your in-laws and aunts, uncles and cousins? How about friends? Do you have a ton of acquaintances but want more connected relationships? There are no right or wrong answers here, it's just a marker of what the situation is right now. So, as with physical environment, give your relationship wedge a rating from 1 to 10 with one being we need some new blood around here to 10 being your life is filled beyond measure with the very best relationships and you would change nothing. So now go ahead and color the wedge.

3. **Love:** Okay so while we're feeling all warm and fuzzy now thinking about our friends, let's continue on with love. In this section, I want to talk about not only the love of our spouse or significant other romantic partner, but also about our self-love. Lots of folks, me included, are not in a romantic relationship at the moment. So if you're romantically connected with another person you'll be thinking about two things in this wedge. I want you to think about your satisfaction with your romantic relationship, but I also want you to think about your rela-

tionship with yourself. So, only if you have a significant other, I'd like for you to further divide the "love" pie piece down the center to make two wedges. In the first, you'll assess how you feel about your romantic relationship and the second half will be your relationship you have with yourself. For those of us without a romantic partner, you just have to concentrate on the relationship with yourself. While that might seem simple, oftentimes it's not. So again fill in the wedge according to your satisfaction level. If you have a romantic partner, a ten might be that "they complete me!" and a one might be "they gotta go!" If you're flying solo, a ten might be "I love me and everything about me…" and a one might look like, "how can I get away from me?"

4. **Fun and Recreation:** What do you do in your downtime? How satisfied are you in this area of your life? This is as different for most people as there are different people in this world. Some folks may love to chat or jet set around the globe on vacation, while others are happy sitting on the couch reading a book or binge watching Netflix. Again no right or wrong answers, just think about your downtime and how satisfied you are with how you are spending it. A rating of one might be what downtime? I'm always working! A ten might be I wouldn't change a thing.

5. **Health:** So this one isn't really about how you're feeling health wise. It's about how you're feeling about your health. You might be tempted to say, "Well, I feel fine" and score yourself a big old 10, but what I'm asking you is how you're feeling about your health? Are you taking care of yourself? Are you stressed out? How's your diet? Do you get regular check-ups? Put a number on it 1 to 10 where one is "please help me" and 10 is never better.

6. **Personal Growth:** Who was it that said if you're not growing you're dying? I know I heard it from Tony Robbins, but not sure if he originated it. It's true, though. If we do not continue to grow and learn

and expand horizons, we will lose our ability to do so. So this section pertains not only to your personal self-growth and education but also your spirituality. How satisfied do you feel in this area of your life where one equals I know nothing about nothing, and 10 equals I know everything I need to know, thank you very much.

7. **Career:** Okay so now we're getting down to it. How are you feeling about what you do every day for living? Simply put here, a ten might be that you feel almost guilty cashing your check because you love what you do so much! A one might be that you hit the snooze button seven times before you drag yourself out of bed – you'd prefer a root canal to having to spend another eight hours in that hellhole! This section also pertains to you stay at home moms and dads! Raising children is one of the damn most important jobs on the planet - you just happen to do it for free! So, for you folks a one might be "oh my God where's the Calgon? Take me away!" to a 10 "God made me to be a parent."

8. **Money:** Rounding out our wheel is the money wedge - your finances and how you feel about them. You might make a lot of money but still not be satisfied and think more will make you happier, while someone else is making minimum wage and is happy with what they have. All that depends on where you are in your life and what you're looking for, so a one here might be "What money? I'm fighting the cat for dinner tonight!" A 10 could mean I have more than I need or can possibly use.

Okay – finished? That was a lot of thinking and reflecting!! Now what does it all mean?

Well take a look at your wheel. Does it look something like this?

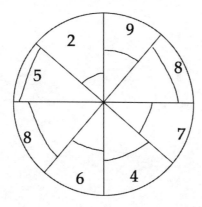

Look at it and imagine that it was an actual wheel - like one on a bicycle. Would you be able to get around on that? Maybe you could if the air was a little low all around, but if some areas are really out of whack that might be a bent rim or something else that really requires some attention. So, with that said, this is just a reflection of how you're feeling right now. Your lower rated wedges might be a place where you want to begin working to improve, but it's not a requirement. For instance, your love-life might be sorely lacking but you're willing to put that on the back burner, at least for the moment, to focus on and build your career. Maybe your career is a snooze-fest and you would like nothing better than to be starting your own business or breaking free to try something different but your significant other is in their last year of medical school and you have to be there emotionally and possibly financially until they finish. Maybe you have some health concerns that you just have to take care of while you still have a steady coming in. There's no rhyme or reason for picking a place to start. What matters is that you start somewhere. I broke some of the chapters in this book into the sections of the wheel, so that you can skip around if you'd like, however, all of the wedges contain information pertinent to your happiness, so don't stray too far!

So, let's get started…

CHAPTER THREE

Physical Environment

Often our moods can be greatly influenced by our physical environment. Look around you, whether you are at home, at work or in your car – how does your current surroundings make you feel? Our physical environment impacts us both internally and externally. Luckily it is very easy to adjust for the better and increase our happiness levels exponentially.

I'm going to start with the subject of clutter, because it seems to be a common complaint with just about everyone I talk to. We all seem to be surrounded by it…whether in our homes, our offices our email box, voicemails or all the stuff that is rattling around in our heads.

One of the reasons that vacations are so relaxing is because we are away from most of our stuff and the responsibilities that come with it. You don't have to worry about all sorts of projects and chores around the house and can just relax and not feel guilty that you're not out mowing the lawn, you can just enjoy the space you are in. You're away from appointments, work and (hopefully) being reachable. This allows you to focus on the people with you.

While we probably can't replicate this feeling of vacation all the time, what we can do is reduce the clutter in our lives and simplify things. This then allows us to focus on what's important and what makes us happy. Here are just a couple of simple ideas to help you start decluttering.

Let's start simply with your home. If you really want to dig deep, there are a ton of books, blogs and magazine articles dedicated to the art of decluttering. While it isn't easy, what it boils down to is going through your home, one room, area, closet or draw at a time and finding things you no longer need or want. These things can be thrown out or given away. The idea is that in the end you are left with things you appreciate and a lot more clear space that's more relaxing to live in and easier to keep clean and organized.

Next, take a look at your computer – your calendar specifically. What are the activities and obligations in your life? Being busy makes us feel pro-ductive, but often the best use of our time is to cut out all the extra stuff that really isn't necessary and that doesn't bring you joy. Don't be afraid to be ruthless and even a little impolite at times. Feeling obligated shouldn't be a good enough reason why you're doing something. Get rid of it and then use the gained time to do things that help you relax, get ahead, and most importantly – make you happy!

Last but not least, it's time to declutter your brain. It's amazing how much "junk" we let build up in there. We all have this running list of things we should do, ideas for future projects, what to cook, what to shop for etc. What we don't realize is how much brain power that kind of thinking takes up. The best way to deal with it is to do a "brain dump". Get out a piece of paper and just start writing it all down. Everything that you have in your head that you think you need to remember – from the book that you want to read next to what to cook for dinner tomorrow, to the meeting you need to schedule at work. Write it all down. Don't judge, don't edit and don't try to organize it. All of that can come later. For now write it down and get it out of your head.

As I am writing this book, an idea for my next book came up. I'm excited for that new project, but knew I needed to finish this one first. However, as I was progressing on this book, one particular chapter of the new book kept popping into my head…all different things I wanted to say, ideas etc. I kept pushing it to the side, because I wanted to focus, focus, focus….but then I just couldn't do it anymore. I couldn't get these thoughts out of my head, and it was affecting EVERYTHING I was doing, not just writing this book. So, I just sat down, and wrote what was in my head…I just had to GET IT OUT! Now that it's out, I am back to concentrating on my current project.

When you're done decluttering, take notice of how much lighter and happier you feel with each area of your life. It's not easy and can be time consuming, but definitely worthwhile and something you should do regularly.

Now that your space is decluttered, take stock of your surroundings. Does your place need a little sprucing up? You know you can do a lot to brighten up your space without spending a ton of money or effort. I currently have carpet in my bedroom, and one of my favorite things is when the carpet is freshly vacuumed. On the weekend, I will launder my sheets and put them back on the bed. I will pick up around my room and my last step is to run the vacuum over the carpet. I love seeing the marks in the carpet made by the vacuum! It didn't cost me anything, but it makes me so very happy.

No matter where I have lived, I always decorate my place nicely. I love to spend time at home, so it has to be nice. Often, I didn't have a lot of money, so I decorated from places like Kmart and Walmart and Target. A can of paint can be bought for under $20, and can literally transform a room. Some new throw pillows for the sofa, a bright comforter for your bed…or maybe it's just some fresh flowers you pick up at the supermarket. This is your space. You are special, so your place should be too!

Don't forget your work environment either. We spend the bulk of our waking hours at the office, so we might as well enjoy our environment.

Make sure your computer wires are tamed. Clean your keyboard and mouse – getting rid of the remnants of last week's lunch! If you're one of those people that like to have pictures of your spouse and family on your desk, it's time to bring in some new pictures – or move them around. Maybe buy yourself some new desk supplies. I prefer shopping in Staples to Bloomingdale's and will occasionally change up my desk set. I'll buy the matching stapler, tape holder and pencil cup. I'll buy pretty folders or binders. If your work is a chore (I hope not) what tools you use shouldn't be. Spice up your space!

Most of us drive to and from to work, so your car gets a lot of wear and tear. I always leave the house with coffee in the morning, and inevitably spill it in the cup holder. Because my life is so busy and hectic, I don't get a chance to clean it as often as I would like. Take a good look at your ride – does it need a little attention? If you can afford to do it, don't just get it washed, get it detailed. It might cost you a hundred bucks – depending on the kind of car you have, but when you get it back you will feel like you got a new car! I try to do that once each year. A lot of bigger office parks have someone come to the parking lot and they will wash or detail your car while you work. How's that for multi-tasking! Once my car is clean inside and out, I'll but it a little present…usually it's a new gadget or an audio book. Maybe it's a cell phone holder or new funky mats for the floor. Even a new air freshener can make a difference. If you can't afford to get it detailed, a good wash or even the drive through can make a difference.

Do you think you would feel happier if you leave your spiffed up desk at your job in the evening and you get into your nice clean car, that has that new car smell or pina colada air freshener, and you drive home to your beautifully decluttered home, where you can relax in peace and comfort for the rest of the evening? It sounds blissful to me, and I think you will feel happier too!

CHAPTER FOUR

Family & Friends

Like it or not, we are social creatures who crave human connections. It's something else that is hardwired into our brains because we need to work together to ensure the survival of our species. We have to work together to make that happen. It only makes sense then that forming and maintaining those connections has an internal reward built in. On the flip side, when we spend too much time isolated and alone, we start to feel sad and depressed.

It is our interaction with other people more than anything else, which brings us happiness. It isn't the amount of money we make or have stashed away in a bank account. It isn't the fancy house, the fancy car and all the stuff we accumulate over the years. What makes us truly happy is spending time and sharing experiences with other people.

Of course, not every single person makes us happy. We all have to deal with plenty of people we don't particularly enjoy spending time with. We may be working on a project at the office with some of them. They may be our neighbors, or someone who attends the same yoga class as you. Some folks we are ambivalent about, and others we'd rather not spend time with at all given the choice, yet all of these relationships have their benefits. I firmly believe that everyone comes into your life for a reason. They're either a blessing or a lesson. Some people will be with us forever, and others will come and go.

If your goal is to be happy, then you should surround yourself with people that make you happy. Moods are contagious. If you're around a bunch of sad and depressed people, you'll start to feel down. If, on the other hand, you are in a group of happy people, you can't help but start to smile.

Does this mean that you should shut all people who aren't happy out of your life? Of course not. We all have important people in our lives whom we love and cherish even if they don't have the sunniest outlook on life. Plus, we all have happier and sadder seasons in our lives. It would be horrible if we avoided loved ones – or they avoided us – during tough times.

That said, there may be people in your life that it's time to let go of. They have served their purpose in your life – even if you still love and care for them. It may be a past romantic relationship, that although you said you'd "remain friends" becomes too difficult when you see them around town or on Facebook. It's time, for your own happiness to let them go and move on.

A few years ago I was living in California. I had moved there to care for my dad. I took the first job that was offered to me the day after I arrived just to be employed. That, in itself was sad because I had had my own business in North Carolina and had loved it. My previous home, Charlotte, North Carolina, is beautiful and green, and while San Diego is an awesome place to live, where I was living was just brown and old. When I first moved out there, I didn't really know anyone. I had family out there, but I had not even met them until I moved there.

I would try to make myself feel better by calling back home often to keep my connection with my friends. I would call one friend, in particular, quite frequently. Jody (not her real name) and I had been relatively good friends. We both had our own businesses in their early stages, and we struggled sometimes, but we could always laugh about our struggles. When she was having a really hard time, I would be her cheerleader and try to lift her up. If I was having a hard time, she would try to make me feel better by telling me how much worse her problem or life was. I was distracted from my own problems to help her with hers.

After a while, I began to notice the pattern. She was never my cheerleader. There was never any advice or sympathy. All she did was turn it around to make it about her. If I tried to turn it back to me by complaining about my job, she would make me feel guilty by saying "Just be thankful you have a job!" Finally, I got to a point where I just couldn't do it anymore. I eventually stopped taking her calls and eventually the friendship just died off. I think they call it "ghosting" now. It was a drastic move, but at the time it was literally for my own survival.

There is a reason that people say that you are or will be the average of the five people you spend the most time around. Take a look at who you are spending your time with. Are they happy and positive people, or negative and draining. Who is the most positive person you know, and when was the last time you spoke to them? Just as we declutter our homes, sometimes it's time to say goodbye to people in our lives. It doesn't have to be as drastic as what I did with Jody, and maybe, by having a conversation with the person, you might be able to salvage the relationship – but sometimes, and I believe you will know when that time is, it's time to let some people go. You can wish them love and happiness (even silently) and then release them from your life.

Maybe it's time to add some new friends to your group. If you do, make sure you pick them wisely, if you want to grow as a person and if your goal is happiness. Spend as much time as you can with these happy, positive people.

Above all, make sure you nurture those important close relationships with family and friends. Those connections will help boost your happiness and make you feel like you're part of something bigger that gives meaning to your life. When we are with people we love and whose company we enjoy, we get a lot of joy, satisfaction, and happiness out of those interactions. We have evolved into beings who crave the mental, social and physical connections. There's a reason why almost everyone appreciates a heartfelt hug.

Spending time with people who love and encourage us and those who challenge us and make us push harder, help us grow as human beings. We get better when we have cheerleaders and mentors around us.

I think this is the perfect time to address technology as it pertains to our relationships. The first thing I want to say is that I absolutely LOVE technology. I love gadgets! I have multiple iPhones, computers and tablets. I can't imagine not having them in my life. What did we ever do without them? I love that I am never more than a phone call, text or email away from someone that needs to reach me. I love that I am able to take my business on the road with me. I also love social media – especially Facebook. It is such a great tool for keeping in touch or getting back in touch we people we lost contact with. It can be a fabulous teaching tool or a pastime when you are alone and lonely. What it shouldn't become, though, is a replacement for the human connection we need – the family and friends that are within arm's reach.

We are never NOT connected. We take our phones in the car, to the store, to the bathroom and to bed with us. It's probably the last thing we look at before we shut off the lights to sleep and the first thing we check when we open our eyes in the morning. I know because it is exactly what I do. I'm not here asking you to give them up – that would be CRAY CRAY! I am asking you to lessen up.

I have been witness, on more than one occasion, of people spending time together – but not actually speaking or interacting with each other. A family of four at dinner at a nice restaurant. Not one of them said one word to each other...they were all on their devices. The other day I saw a mother with her precious baby girl sitting on a blanket on the grass below my balcony. The baby was looking at the mom, but the mom was looking at her phone.

20

The baby started to crawl away, off the blanket. The mom, without looking up, just stuck out her leg and created a barrier that the baby couldn't cross. It was so sad. I wanted to yell down to her and tell her that she is going to blink and that little girl will be heading off to college.

It used to be that you would leave work at night and come back in the morning or after the weekend and resume. In an emergency, they might call you at home. Now our bosses can reach us 24/7 – and most of them do! Even when it's not an emergency. We need to set boundaries of when we're available and when we're offline.

My friend got married last year. As she sat in the chair having her hair and makeup done, she was also participating in conference calls for work. She couldn't even experience the joy of her own wedding day preparations. Finally, her brother came into the room, and said "That's enough!" and took the phone from her hand and threw it across the room. Boundaries.

I've heard it said that our devices keep us closer to those farthest from us, but keep us farther from those closest to us. How true is that statement? If you're home alone and there's no one to hang with – by all means, grab that phone and watch all the crazy cat videos your heart desires. But if you are home and sitting down to dinner with your family…put your phone in another room and ask them to do the same. Have an actual conversation. Ask about each other's day. Take a good look at them. Tell them you love them. Be present. They, or you, will be gone before you know it. You will never regret an "I Love You" said, but you will have plenty of regrets over the ones you didn't get a chance to say.

When you are on your deathbed, I want you to be looking up into the faces of people that adore you, not the bored put-upon faces of those you ignored while you were busy fulfilling your boss's every need…he most likely not going to be one of the faces that will be sharing your last moments with you.

I promise you…happiness is NOT in those devices. Keep them, use them, love them – but don't let them replace the people in your life. Stay connected…by disconnecting.

Need more happiness in your life? Check out my website , www.gohappyyourself.com for tips, tools and ideas for making your happiness garden grow.

CHAPTER FIVE

Love

I don't think there is a more beautiful word in the English language. That loving feeling is the best feeling in the world, yet that one small word encompasses a wide range of emotion. While you may love ice cream or those new peep toe booties you just bought, the feeling is nothing compared to that of when you first held your child in your arms or when you said "I do" to your spouse. It is also a bank that keeps refilling itself - the more you spend, the more love you give this world, the more you will get back. We would not have the problems in this world today if everyone acted more from love.

For instance, I'm writing this chapter on a flight from North Carolina to San Diego. It was an early flight for which I had to get up very early, as did the other 184 passengers on board, and the crew who were up even earlier than the passengers. Add to that all the airport personnel who might be at the end of the very long shift or are also up before the crack of dawn like the rest of us. Some folks are traveling with young children and some are handicapped. Stressful to be sure, and for myself nowhere near enough caffeine, Yet everyone - every single person on this flight is so pleasant. The flight attendants are friendly and engaging with the passengers. The passengers are engaging with each other. The guy in the seat next to me got up and helped several others put their suitcases in the overhead compartment. No one was punched in the face or dragged screaming from their seats off the plane. This is how it is when you act from love.

So this not only pertains to your relationship with your significant other it also directly relates to your relationship with yourself. Often we are most critical and self-loathing of ourselves. We put ourselves down for the most inconsequential things and then continue to beat ourselves to a bloody pulp over it. Does this sound familiar, "Dammit, I forgot to pick up the dry cleaning when I was out! What a stupid idiot! Why didn't I write that on my list? What a jerk! – or "Oh my God I can't believe I ate that ice cream and a piece of cake on top of those two slices of pizza! What a pig! I'm disgusting!" I'm sure you've said, if not those exact things to yourself, you said something similar. Yet if it was your significant other that forgot to pick up the dry cleaning, I don't think you would be nearly that harsh. Probably more like "No worries, honey, I'll run out and get it - or we can get it tomorrow." Would you call your best friend a disgusting pig when she told you how she binged? Or would you show her some love and encouragement? I'm thinking most probably the latter.

Why are we kinder to complete strangers then we are to ourselves why is it easier to tell others we love them but we can't say we love ourselves? When we are kinder to ourselves, accept ourselves with all our faults and love ourselves unconditionally, we open the floodgates to increasing love in all of our relationships. When you love and accept yourself your relation-ship with your significant other is greatly improved. Many of the problems in our relationships are due to perceived slights, hurt feelings, etc. Often those events are seen through our own lens of discontent with ourselves. So this happened…after I got married I gained a bit of weight. My husband and I had a formal event to go to, and I had borrowed this beautiful black lace dress from a friend. It looked fantastic on and I thought it made me look slimmer because it was black. When my husband saw me his only comment was "I thought you were going to wear the blue dress?" From there my mind exploded with questions and insecurities – "Does he not like this dress?, Do I look fat? Will his family not approve of the dress?" I never voiced these questions out loud, I just went to the event feeling self-conscious and sad. I had a terrible time. By the time we got home, I had silently worked myself up into quite a state as I took off the dress. As I went to hang the stupid thing back in the closet, I saw my blue dress on the rack and pulled it out to see why my husband preferred that dress. As I did so, something was dangling from the hanger. A beautiful sapphire, diamond and gold necklace, along with a note that said To match your beautiful blue eyes. I love you." Well, the tears started streaming down my face as my husband entered the room. "I thought you were going to wear the blue dress," he said quietly, "and I wanted to surprise you."

He too had spent the evening in disappointment. I asked why he didn't just tell me to wear the blue dress and he told me that he didn't want to push it because he knew I was sensitive about my weight, and didn't want me to think the exact things I had been thinking about anyway. Because of my insecurities and self-loathing, both of our evenings were disappointing. Having flaws and accepting them doesn't mean you can't change them, it just means that you can be happier as you bring about your change. It's like getting a bad haircut. You can hide out in your house and cry, wear a hat, buy a wig, or you can just spike up that hair and wear it like a boss. It is going to take the same exact amount of time to grow out no matter which attitude you choose, so why wouldn't you choose the one that makes you happy.

I know you opened this chapter expecting to find out how your love life increases your happiness – or vice versa, but the message that I really want to get across to you here is that it is your love affair with YOURSELF that makes your relationship with your significant other more pleasurable and thereby increasing your happiness.

How can we expect anyone to love us if we don't love ourselves? Why do we feel so unworthy? I'll tell you a story that will illustrate how accepting yourself can change things in your life – actually change your life.

I'll stick with this weight thing…I know this is a touchy subject for a lot of people – especially women. I have struggled with my weight for most of my life. As you can tell from the incident with my husband and I above, it's always been a sore subject for me. I had tried just about every diet known to man. I would lose weight and then gain it back. Time and time again. Each time I would gain the weight back, I would feel like a failure, which just chipped and chipped away at my already low self-confidence.

But, as you get older, something changes, and when I turned 41 I decided for my birthday that year I was going to stop dieting. I wasn't giving myself a license to binge, but I was not going to put myself through the torture of facing the scale every morning. This is a long story in itself, so I'll just cut to the chase. I felt free and liberated. It was an exhilarating feeling. I enjoyed it for all of 6 weeks, when a very dear friend begged me to go on a diet with her as she tried to lose weight for her upcoming wedding.

Long story short, I did it because she asked me to, but when I went on this particular diet, I wasn't putting my whole future happiness on the line. The diet called for a two week "induction" period, so I promised my friend I would commit to that period. If I didn't want to stay on it after that, she would be cool with it. It turns out that I stayed on the diet for four years straight and lost in excess of 80 pounds. It changed my life. I was thinner than I had ever been in my life. I was thinner than my friends. I not only looked great, I felt great. I was happy…until …

Until I realized that nothing really had changed. All of the things that I had been telling myself would happen – if I only lost weight…didn't actually happen. I was "dating" a guy who didn't deserve me because I thought it was all I deserved. I thought I would meet the man of my dreams, my soulmate when I lost my weight. I thought my life would be like I had seen in the movies…but it wasn't. I had spent all those years waiting, only to find out that was the problem…it wasn't the weight that was making me unhappy – it was the <u>wait</u>!

When I had first lost all that weight, I went out dancing with two friends. I was excited to go out with this new dress I had bought that looked really hot on me. One of the other girls was thin as well and she, too was dressed to the nines. The third girl, was quite a bit heavier. She was dressed very nicely, in clothing that pretty much covered her up. We did have a great time, but let's just say that I didn't get the attention that I thought I would in that dress, and neither did my other (thin) friend. Our heavier friend met someone that night and continued her evening with him as we two headed home.

It doesn't matter what you weigh, what color your eyes are, what your hair looks like – or even if you have hair. What matters is how you feel about those things...and really do those things matter? When someone falls in love with – really falls in love with us – they don't fall for all that crap. They fall for the person inside.

Go fall in love with yourself. When you wake up in the morning and head to the bathroom, look at yourself, bed head and all – look yourself deep in the eye. Say out loud "I Love You (insert your name)". It is going to feel very awkward and you will not even believe it even if you do say it. Keep doing that every time you pass a mirror, but especially first thing in the morning. Do it every day, and really mean it when you say it. When it starts sinking in, you will feel the difference. You will start treating yourself better. You will stop the negative chatter in your head...and you will increase your happiness level. It will also have a ridiculously positive impact on your romantic relationship, because when we are happy with ourselves, it becomes amazingly sexy and attractive to our partners...go try it and see for yourself!

CHAPTER SIX

Fun and Recreation

We lead busy lives and have all sorts of obligations as parents, professionals, and friends. It's easy to lose yourself in everything that has to be done in any given week. Come the weekend, there are chores to be done, errands to be run, kids to be shuffled around. The two days goes by before you know it and you return to work on Monday less rested than you were after working a full week.

Even our vacations can be hectic. Trying to cram as much into the one or two weeks as we can. Do you even take a vacation? As a society, we are so connected, that even if we manage to get away, we tend to make ourselves available for that ever important conference call or to answer a couple or couple dozen emails.

Many of us don't take vacations because we can't afford it. We live in a material society where it seems that our main goal seems to be to acquire more stuff. We buy bigger cars, bigger houses, and of course, lots and lots of stuff to fill those houses. We seem to think that we can buy happiness by having more "stuff." All these things have to be taken care of and with bigger houses and cars comes bigger maintenance issues and repair costs. We've been living this way in the Western world for quite some time. We have to pay for these possessions by putting more and more time in at work.

So what's the answer? Well, in the search for happiness there is a new trend of owning less, and living simpler, more minimalistic lives. We see it in the trend towards minimalism, tiny houses, and in the success of books like "The Life-Changing Magic of Tidying Up." There must be something to this idea of owning less and focusing less on buying and owning things.

Does this mean that to be happy we have to give away all our stuff and move into a tiny house or apartment? Well not necessarily, although I think as we get older it seems to be quite appealing to do just that. But, how about, instead of accumulating more stuff, we try focusing on experiences. Instead of buying a fancy car, new furniture or a set of golf clubs, take that money and spend it on a fun family trip. Use it to spend quality time with your loved ones and make beautiful memories. Not only will you increase your happiness during the time you're on vacation, you'll also feel such joy as you remember this trip and the time spent with your spouse and kids.

You don't even have to go that far. Vacations are great, but we can't take them all the time, and they aren't always practical. Think of spending quality time instead of buying gifts. Instead of buying another blouse or book for your mom or best friend, take her out on her birthday for lunch and some girl time. Instead of buying your son another electronic gadget, take him and a friend to the ballpark and cheer on your favorite team.

Staycations are very popular now, but as a kid that was all I knew. My father was always working, so we rarely went anywhere. But every Monday during the summer, my mother, aunt and uncle would pile us all in the car and head to the beach. I can recall those days as if they were yesterday. The times spent with my sister and brother, the feel of the salt water drying tightly on my skin, jumping the waves and the crunch of the broken shells beneath our feet as we jumped those waves, the taste of the Italian ices we would sometimes stop for on the way home (I always got cherry!) and the sunburn we would experience when we got home. We carry those memories forever.

Another solution to living a happier and more content life is to learn to live in the moment. You don't want to miss out on all the amazing little things life has in store for you because you're too busy worrying and agonizing over everything you have to do. The goal for a happier life is to learn to live in the moment. You can start by simply paying attention to what's going on around you right now. Literally stop and smell the roses. Enjoy the people you are spending time with – even if it's for a quick dinner out. Look around and notice the beauty in your surroundings. Each season brings new natural phenomena that can help you stay in the moment and make you happy. Treasure the first few green sprouts at the end of winter, the warm summer day, the crisp fall leaves. Each day, each season and each year has amazing treasures to offer if you take the time to stay in the moment and notice them.

Don't forget to include some time for you to spend on yourself. Sometimes you need to treat yourself to a little "me" time. Don't feel guilty about it. In the end, it makes you a better parent, a better colleague and a better friend. We all need to recharge and we need to do something just for ourselves on a regular basis and it doesn't have to be complicated.

If taking time for yourself to do something that you enjoy and that relaxes you isn't something you're doing right now, figure out what you may want to do. Maybe it's reading a good book or watching your favorite TV show. Maybe it's getting back into a hobby you used to enjoy. Maybe it's as simple as having 10 minutes to sit by yourself and think, or thumb through a magazine. Maybe it's taking a nap!

Your first task is to find out what it is you want to do for yourself. Time to do what you enjoy is always a favorite. It doesn't have to be a lot of time and it doesn't have to involve anything complicated. Sure, a trip to the beach by yourself for a week would be great, but if that's not an option, curling up on the couch with a nice cup of tea and a good book will do.

Treating yourself to a new haircut, a manicure and/or pedicure or a massage may be another option. If you have kids that follow you from room to room, it can be as simply as doing the grocery shopping alone and picking up a favorite treat that you don't have to share.

The point I'm trying to make here is to trade things for experiences and that it is okay to treat yourself and do something for the sole purpose of making you happy. While a piece of chocolate and a bike ride with your kids may not seem like that big of a deal in the grand scheme of things, making memories and treating yourself well and caring for yourself can have a huge impact on the rest of your day and how you treat those around you. Give it a try. Go make a memory. Go do something good for yourself.

CHAPTER SEVEN

Health

Happiness and your health – both physical and mental, go hand in hand. The most interesting idea here is that being happy and making an effort to increase your happiness can have a very positive effect on your overall health and well-being.

You've probably heard the saying Laughter is the best medicine. It turns out that there is a lot of truth to that statement. If you google comedian Norm Cousins, you can see how he was able to control his very chronic and painful disease with a regular regimen of laughter.

Being happy, content and even laughing out loud is a great way to reduce pain. The next time you have a backache, turn on a funny movie or simply make yourself laugh and see if it makes you feel better. Being happy is also good for your heart. People who are happy tend to have lower blood pressure and lower heart rates. Both decrease the risk of heart disease in the long run.

One thing that can kill your happiness is stress. It's hard to be happy when you're stressed out. I know I don't have to tell you that. I'm sure you've experienced it for yourself. Think back on high stress situations like missing your flight on your way to vacation, or planning your wedding. Both should be joyful events and may start out that way, but things can get overwhelming really quickly. Hopefully it all works out and you get to enjoy your special time, but chances are you weren't too happy when you were stressed out. Stress can suck the happiness and joy right out of us. The secret is to increase your happiness while reducing your stress levels.

Some ways we can decrease our stress levels is by:

» Getting enough sleep. If you can, try and get 7-8 hours of good sleep each night. I know that's easier said than done – just ask any parent of a newborn – but when we don't get a good rest, our bodies are in a constant state of stress trying to make up for the lack of sleep.

Sleep helps us relax and gives our mind time to process everything that's been happening. So stop burning the midnight oil and get some rest. You'll get more done when you're fresh and rested and you'll be less stressed about it.

To help get the best rest while you sleep, try removing or blocking all light sources in your room – windows, clocks, computer and smartphone screens. This seemed like a lot of work and I didn't believe it would make a big difference, so I tried it – and it makes a huge difference. However, I was not prepared to remove all the light sources from my room every single night, so I opted for a sleep mask. It took a night or two to get used to it, but now I can't sleep without it. Another thing I tried and have now implemented into my sleep routine is to play a hypnosis or a guided meditation CD. I have to tell you, I am having the best sleep of my life! Another thing that I have just heard about, but have not tried yet is placing a Himalayan sea salt lamp in the room. I don't know exactly what it's supposed to do, but so many people are using them for sleep issues, that I wanted to include that piece of info here for you. They seem to be pretty affordable. I have seen them at Bed Bath and Beyond.

» Get some exercise – without a doubt, and this is coming from the girl who HATES exercise, but it is the #1 way to relieve stress. Start moving and burn that stress right out of your system. If you can do it outside, even better. The fresh air and sunshine will do wonders. Just don't do it too close to bedtime. You will be too energized to sleep!

» Take some time for yourself. We have crazy lives and we always seem to be focused on the needs of others that it's easy to forget about putting our own needs first. I know it's hard, but try to find a little "me" time each day. It doesn't have to be much – even 10 minutes spent relaxing and doing something completely selfish can be a great way to decompress and destress.

» Meditate – meditation is a great way to keep stress at bay. If you've never meditated, start with just a minute or two. Trying to meditate for 30 minutes or an hour your first time out will stress you out and defeat the purpose. Once you get better at meditating and get in the habit of doing it daily, you can draw on the techniques you've learned when you encounter a particularly stressful situation. It is a great tool to have in your happiness toolbox!

» Don't sweat it – It's easy to get caught up in little things that stress us out each day. Getting cut off in traffic or getting to work to find out your co-worker called in sick and you have to pick up the slack. We can choose to get bent out of shape over every little thing or we can choose to not make a big deal out of it and use that small, insignificant stuff to practice seeing the positive side of things. Getting cut off may have slowed you down and thereby you avoided a ticket – or an accident. Maybe you learned a new skill or met a new friend while filling in for your co-worker.

Dr. Wayne Dyer said –"when you change the way you look at things, the things you look at change." Try to look on the bright side of every situation and watch your happiness level increase.

HAPPINESS AND NUTRITION

It should come as no surprise that what we choose to put in our bodies can and does have a direct impact on our mood – and thereby our happiness levels. It is really interesting to learn how much the food we eat can affect our mood. I think it's no accident that since the advent of lots of processed food with added sugar in the Western diet, depression and other mood disorders have dramatically risen. We constantly look for different ways to increase our happiness when the simplest solution may be to change what we eat.

Before we dive in, I'd like to make this point. At first glance, it may seem that eating certain foods like fresh fruits and vegetables, fresh seafood and high-quality chocolate are things that only rich people, wealthy people – or just someone with more resources than you buys and eats regularly. You may be tempted then to believe that these foods are out of your reach(financially) and that the people that are eating them are happier because they can afford the fancy fruit. It's actually not the case, and studies and analysis has been done to ensure that there is an actual CAUSAL relationship between certain foods and happiness

Let's look at a couple of key ingredients and nutrients that have been shown to directly affect our mood. Ask any female and she will tell you that foods like chocolate and wine can greatly improve your mood… but let's go over a couple more that can have a positive impact on your mood and therefore your overall happiness.

COFFEE

I'm gonna start right off the bat with my absolute favorite. Coffee is amazing! It is one of the main sources of antioxidants in the typical western diet. Additionally, it has plenty of caffeine (yay!) which will help you get motivated to get out and do stuff. Taking action and getting outside can both have great positive effects on your levels of happiness.

35

Coffee will also increase dopamine and serotonin transmission within a few minutes of consumption, helping you feel better right away. The next time you feel low and blue, brew yourself a strong cup of coffee and watch your mood improve. I'm not low and blue right now, but I'm going to get another cup!

CHOCOLATE

If there was ever a perfect food group, I think chocolate would be it. Chocolate is very interesting. It includes polyphenols – mood boosting chemicals that will instantly make you feel calmer and happier. The darker the chocolate the better the effect. Of course the antioxidants from the cocoa beans and the amazing flavor of good quality dark chocolate doesn't hurt either...

FRUITS AND VEGETABLES

Well you knew I was getting here eventually. We already know that fruits and vegetables are good for our health. But did you know that they can also greatly enhance your mood? They absolutely do – and for a variety of reasons. The first is that they contain plenty of vitamin C. Fresh fruits and veggies are our main source of this crucial vitamin. Not only does it give your immune system a boost, it's also an important building block for making dopamine, the happiest compound in our body.

Of course it isn't the only part of the fruits and veggies that help. Many of the vitamins, minerals and phytonutrients that we'll talk about in the rest of this chapter can be found in various fruits and vegetables.

As with coffee, they are also full of antioxidants, which play an important role in reducing inflammation in the body (among other things!). That has a powerful effect on your overall well-being and mood. Eating about 8 servings of fruit and veggies a day will have a noticeable effect on your mood.

NUTS ABOUT NUTS – WALNUTS IN PARTICULAR

Nuts and seeds, walnuts in particular include high levels of alpha-linoleic acid (ALA). Low levels of ALA have been associated with low moods and even depression. This is in part caused by the fact that low levels of ALA decreases the levels of dopamine in your system. Additionally, low levels of ALA tend to increase inflammation throughout your body which has also been shown to aid depression.

Incorporate walnuts, flax and other nuts and seeds high in ALA in your diet and see if it makes a difference. It takes a little while for inflammation to go down, so give it a few weeks and see how you feel.

CLAMS AND OYSTERS

Clams have very high levels of B12 which is another precursor for dopamine in the body. Low levels of B12 have been shown to cause depression. Oysters, on the other hand, are a great source of zinc. Low levels of zinc can cause anxiety, while high levels of zinc can help with depression. In other words, now may be a great time to increase your seafood intake and watch the effect it has on your mood.

YOGURT AND KEFIR

Yogurt and Kefir are an interesting food group. They work by improving our gut bacteria, which in turn has a big impact on inflammation, digestion, and the immune system. Incorporating them into your diet regularly can have a very positive effect on your mood. Make sure you consume yogurt with live cultures and the less sugar in each – the better.

In addition, certain vitamins and minerals are particularly good at enhancing mood. If you feel like there's a lack of them in your system, it might be a good idea to supplement with them and see if it helps your mood. If you're deficient in magnesium for example, it can take a while to replenish this through diet alone. Taking a high-quality magnesium supplement can help you improve your mood faster.

VITAMIN B6 AND B12

Being happy takes energy and a key ingredient in making sure we get the energy we need from our foods are B vitamins. Both of these B vitamins are important for the production of dopamine in your system and they also help in converting food into useable energy for your body. This whole group of micronutrients is crucial in how energized we feel. A good complex B vitamin supplement can be a great addition to your diet. Make sure you get plenty to feel your best. Try it and see if you don't start to feel more energized and happier right away.

VITAMIN C

Vitamin C is an important building block for dopamine as well and it gives your immune system a boost. Supplement, particularly in the winter time when it's harder to maintain adequate levels of vitamin C in the body. Of course, eating plenty of fresh fruits and veggies will help as well.

VITAMIN D

We then to get the blues more in winter when we can't get outside and get some sun. A big reason for this drop in mood is a lack of vitamin D. With the advent of strong sunscreen and a global health policy that warns us of sun exposure and cautions us to cover up or wear sunscreen, it's no wonder that vitamin d deficiency has become major problem that also happens to negatively affect our mood.

MAGNESIUM

The soils, particularly in the US are depleted of magnesium, meaning we'll get less and less of this essential mineral in the foods we eat. Magnesium is an important mineral that can help reduce stress, lower blood pressure, and help you sleep better. I don't have to tell you how much of an impact good sleep alone (but I will in a later chapter!) can have on your overall mood and well-being. If you don't believe me, just ask any mother or father of a newborn! Supplement with quality magnesium and see if you don't start to notice a positive difference.

OMEGA-3 FATTY ACIDS

There are two types of omega fatty acids. Omega-3 and Omega-6. In a happy, healthy body, the levels of these two fatty acids will be in balance. Sadly in the western world, we tend to consume way too much omega-6 in processed foods. This imbalance has been shown to directly increase the risk and severity of depression. Boosting your omega-3 fatty acids through a supplement or by eating lots of nuts and seeds can reverse this effect and return you to your regular happy self. While you may want to consider supplementing with some of these nutrients to quickly fill the gap your diet is leaving, a much better long-term strategy is to work on cleaning up your diet. Cutting out foods that can dampen your mood is another good idea. Gluten/wheat and sugar are two substances that have been shown to increase inflammation. As already mentioned, inflammation has been shown to lower our mood and increase our chances of getting depressed. In addition, most processed food include these two ingredients along with the omega-6 fatty acids and various other chemicals and ingredients that aren't great for our health.

One of the best things you can do for your mood is to cut out as much processed food as possible, replacing it with plenty of real food, including fresh fruits and vegetables, seeds and nuts, fermented dairy and seafood. Eat healthy (most of the time) and you'll improve both your physical and emotional health and well-being.

EXERCISE AND HAPPINESS

I briefly touched on exercise above when talking about relieving stress, but even if you are blessed to not have a stressful life, you happiness will increase if you get your body moving. There is a strong link between exercise and an improvement in mood and well-being. When you're having a bad day, or are feeling a bit down in the dumps, the best way to increase your happiness may be to exercise. Give it a try. Go for a 30 minute walk whenever you're feeling depressed and unhappy. You'll notice your mood starting to increase throughout the walk. As you get back, you may notice that you're feeling even happier!

This increase of happiness and well-being after exercise is caused by the release of brain chemicals like endorphins and other mood enhancers. This happens just a few minutes after you work out and the effect can last for a good twelve hours! The second part to the equation is that exercise also helps reduce the levels of stress hormones cortisol and adrenaline in the body. That means you'll instantly feel less stressed. This one-two punch can have a powerful effect on how you feel. Something as simple as a brisk walk can help you feel better almost immediately.

For best results, you'll want to exercise a few times per week. Take some time during your lunch break to go for a walk, or work a quick workout in before you head to work in the morning. It doesn't matter what you do, as long as you start moving around and get that blood pumping. Pick activities that you enjoy and that you will stick with.

So I enjoy walking and bike riding. However, because of my schedule and my caregiving responsibilities, those are not regular options for me. As I mentioned before, I don't like to exercise, but I do most days. I get up ridiculously early (4:00am!) and am on the treadmill at the gym by 4:30am. I tell people I get up and moving before my body even realizes what the heck I'm up to.

The benefits to that are that it gets it out of the way first thing in the morning...which is a two-fold benefit. I don't have to think about it again for the rest of the day. If I didn't get it done, I would be stressed that I won't get to it, and then guilty as I am too tired now to do it. Also, it sets the tone of the day on a positive note and a big accomplishment of have completed something that is not one of my favorite things to do. Plus, I ALWAYS get over that initial "I don't wanna do this" five minutes after I enter the gym.

If you're young, you might have to wait a while for this benefit, but being active and mobile keeps you young. My dad taught me many, many things when I was growing up. I'm still learning from him. My dad's worst problem right now is his mobility. He still gets around with the use of a walker, but it's not easy for him. He has a hard time getting up off his chair and out of the car. I have learned, through watching his struggles, how important it is to take care of the body that we are given.

In addition to the everyday mood booster you get from exercising regularly, there are quite a few additional long term benefits. Exercise is good for your health and you will start to get fitter and even slimmer and more toned if you stick with it. This in turn will improve how you feel and how you feel about yourself. The added confidence can be a great additional mood booster.

My friend Gail wanted to lose weight for an upcoming family wedding. Her work schedule was so hectic that she knew she would never be able to commit to regular gym workouts. She decided to start walking for 20 minutes during her lunch "hour," and she also decided to give up dessert. By the time the wedding rolled around, she had lost 30 pounds! Afterwards she told me that she still continues to walk every day because it makes her feel so good, and helps her mood and stress levels from her job in the afternoon.

Whenever possible, try to get as much exercise as you can outside. Fresh air and sunshine add to the feeling of well-being. Also, if you can do it with someone you enjoy being with, and can share a few laughs with – all the better. It will be so much more enjoyable! Try to come up with some simple things you can start doing right now.

Maybe you CAN go for a walk in the afternoon. Maybe go for a jog after dinner or sign up for a yoga or Pilates class at your local Y or community center. Like sports? What about joining a basketball team…or softball or the bowling league. It doesn't really matter what you choose to do as long as you make it a goal to get more active and move around. Switch it up a bit if you get bored. Arrange a group hike if you get lonely – dust off your bike and tool around town on the weekend. There's a lot of fun ways to move around and enjoy the world around you.

HAPPINESS AND YOUR MENTAL HEALTH

One of the indicators of good mental health can be your level of happiness with your life and the people around you. Do you enjoy being around family and friends? Do you live an active life and have a positive impact on others? Do you like to help out and get great joy from doing things for others? Do you have a positive attitude? Are you a glass half full or half empty person?

Let's face it – life isn't always sunshine and rainbows -and that's a good thing. How boring would it be to only have positive experiences? We need the negative, the sadness, and the disappointments to balance the happiness. They are what make the happy times stand out and shine all the brighter.

That being said, negative thoughts, emotions, and the events and people that cause them are part of life. We have to learn to deal with them and make the best of sad situations to live a happy and content life.

Have you noticed that negative comments and events stick with us much longer, and influence us more than positive ones? I'm sure you've experienced this quite a few times. A positive comment by your teacher or boss is appreciated, but the effects wear off quickly. However, a negative comment seems to stick with you much longer. To this day, I can remember several negative things that my teachers and bosses have said to me… practically word for word. Why is that? It's because our brains have a bias towards negativity. It's measurable and there have been brain scan studies done that show that our brain reacts more strongly to negative stimuli. The big question then is how do we fight against our brain's bias to negativity?

What can we do to make sure negative remarks and criticism don't get us down? The first step is that we realize that there is such a thing. This allows us to take each piece of negativity with a grain of salt. It can be incredibly helpful to acknowledge that our mind and heart may be overreacting about something negative. On the flip side, this knowledge also allows us to make it a point to savor the positivity. Don't dismiss a compliment out of hand… Instead, savor it, think about it, and make it a point to remember it, and allow it to lift you up when negativity brings you down.

There are also a lot of times and situations where we focus too much on the negativity. A little distance, and a little perspective can show us that it's not as bad as we originally thought. Before you allow yourself to wallow in sadness, try your best to step back and look at the situation from a different perspective. Get some sleep, go out for a walk, and come back and look at it again. Try your best to see the positive side of things. Above all, do what you can to outweigh the negativity with the good stuff. Keep a box or file with some of the best positive emails and comments you've gotten. Read through them whenever you need to counteract something negative. As time goes by you'll grow that thicker skin that will protect you from the harshest critics. With that said, we don't get out of this life without facing periods of grief, intense sadness or overwhelm. We all go through hard times. There are periods in our lives where it is hard to find much joy and happiness amid a sea of sadness and overwhelm. We have times when we feel like we're in way over our head and can't think straight. We often feel alone at those times. That causes stress and as we've talked about before, stress kills happiness.

There are also incredibly sad times in our lives. Relationships end and we lose loved ones. There is certainly a time to grieve and we need to process that loss. We also need these sad moments in life to contrast the happier ones. Without sadness, happiness would be meaningless. Think about that for just a moment and let it sink in. If you're never sad, always happy, happiness becomes the new normal – not something to appreciate and strive toward.

During intense periods of sadness and overwhelm, just remember that this is a normal part of life. You need time to process and grieve the situation. It may take time. Don't expect to be able to flip a switch and make it better. There is no timetable on grief and sadness. What helps to know is that it will pass – and that may be just the light at the end of the tunnel that you need to get you through the tough times. We need that little bit of happiness to give us hope.

A couple of things you can do to get you through a rough time is to focus on gratitude. Whenever you feel particularly bad, sad or overwhelmed and don't know where to turn, think about the many people and things in your life that you can be grateful for. If you've recently lost a loved one, be grateful for the time you've had with them and the things you've learned from this special person. If you're stressed out at work or in your own business, be grateful that you're growing and making progress. It may not be easy, but this overwhelm and stress usually means that much better things are ahead.

I find that it's also extremely helpful to find the joy in the little things. Maybe you're not ready to be grateful – and that's okay, too. Instead, pay attention to your surroundings and find a little joy in what's around you. Let that toddler playing in the park put a smile on your face. Enjoy the first warm rays of sunshine in the spring, or notice how beautiful that flower in your garden is. In other words, look around and find a little joy and happiness where you can. Above all, remember that even during hard times, it's okay to find and appreciate these little moments of happiness.

It's when we don't experience this joy and happiness that mental health seems to suffer. At the same time, focusing on happiness and increasing the joy in our lives can help us overcome hard times that have us feeling more depressed and sad than usual. Focusing on being content with what we have helps us become happier and worry less. When we aren't constantly comparing ourselves with others or worrying about things we don't need to be worrying about, we have more time to relax, enjoy, and be happy. It's a powerful strategy.

I just want to take a moment to briefly touch on the difference between being a little blue or being depressed and suffering from true depression. While the lines can be a little blurry at times, there is a difference. Nutrition, exercise and changing your attitude will all help, but if you are suffering from deep depression, please, please seek medical advice. There are deep underlying issues, and brain chemical imbalances that you won't be able to rectify or overcome by working on increasing your happiness.

Schedule a visit with your doctor and work with your medical team to figure out what's going on and how you can work your way out of the depression. Then and only then, come back to this book and use the tips in these pages to increase your happiness and more.

CHAPTER EIGHT

Personal **Growth**

While I title this chapter Personal Growth, it also covers Spirituality. I understand that you and I might not worship the same god. You may not worship anyone or anything at all, but it is my hope that you do believe in a power greater than yourself. If that does not resonate with you either, you may still find some little tidbits in the personal growth discussion.

Although I was raised as a good Catholic girl from Brooklyn, I am not a fan of organized religion. So I would not consider myself religious but would definitely categorize myself as spiritual. I don't doubt the presence of God in my life. He (or she) has shown himself to me time and time again. We could discuss this for weeks, but this chapter is about how spirituality can bring you closer or add to your happiness.

How do you feel when you are with a group of very good friends, or with your close family members? Chances are you feel connection, you feel love, you feel included. You feel good – happy even. Your family and friends are your rock. That is what it feels to be spiritually connected. You feel like you are part of something so much greater than yourself. Almost like you can do anything, because someone has your back.

I used to reach for my spirituality only when I was in trouble. "Dear

God, please help me through this problem." And he did…and then I never prayed again…until the next problem. God – I'm using that because it is what my belief is, but please include whatever force it is that you believe in – God always came through for me. Why? I cannot answer that question. Surely there were people praying for things that prayed every day, yet God ALWAYS had my back. Sometimes he didn't deliver what I was praying for, instead he delivered what I needed – not what I wanted.

So, how do you get connected to Spirit, God, the Universe…whatever… it's so very easy. Be quiet. Get quiet. Some people call it meditating. I call it "shut the hell up." You may be praying day in and day out for things or for help, but how do you know when God is talking to you? Your answers are in the quiet. Prayers are your way of speaking to God. Meditating is God's way of speaking back to you. The problem is that we live in such a fast paced world. We keep going and going. We have no down time. We talk to people on the phone as we drive to and from work. We answer emails standing in line at the post office. We are texting before we fall asleep. Our brains never rest.

I started meditating by accident about ten years ago I was going through a bad time. I didn't know how I was going to resolve my issue. It was financial, and there was really no one I could turn to for help. I had a deadline where I needed to have a lump sum of money. It was within days of that deadline with no money and no idea how to get it. As clear as if it happened yesterday, I remember sitting on my balcony and looking out over the wooded area below. It was a secluded space and the only sounds were my breathing and the wind moving through the trees. I was contemplating my problem as I stared at the different trees. I consciously remember thinking that there must be a solution. I thought the same God that made these beautiful trees also made me, that I had to have within me what I needed to figure this out. Then I closed my eyes and became silent and just breathed.

With that, I can't explain it, but all of a sudden I just KNEW what I had to do. It was a KNOWING. It didn't pop in my head like an idea – like hey! What if I try this? It was just all of a sudden I KNEW – like I knew my own name. Sure enough, I did what I knew and solved my problem. Now I connect whenever I can.

Meditation is a state of thoughtless awareness. It's not easy to do – especially at first – because we are constantly on overdrive – that's why they refer to it as a "meditation practice" . You practice until you can reach that state of mind easily and effortlessly. As you progress, meditating will help you concentrate, contemplate and give you more control over your mind and thoughts.

There are all sorts of different ways to meditate. You can focus on your breathing, other "gurus" will have you focus on your body. You can do it in complete silence or while listening to soft music or white noise. You can even work through a recorded guided meditation.

If you're new to meditating, a simple guided meditation may be your best bet. There are plenty of recordings online, on YouTube and there are even meditation apps you can download right to your smartphone. Some are free, while others are paid guided meditations. Listen to a few to find the right fit for you.

If you want to give this a try without downloading or spending any money, give this basic meditation exercise a try. Start by laying down comfortably on your back. Keep your hands on the side and relax. Close your eyes and breathe naturally. Notice how the breath moves your body and try to focus your mind on each exhalation and inhalation. If your mind starts to wander, bring it back to your breath. Aim for a few minutes to begin with – even ONE minute. Don't feel bad if you find yourself nodding off. Meditation can be very relaxing and a great way to help you get to sleep.

With practice, you will be able to meditate for longer periods of time. Experiment with techniques and lengths of meditation until you find what works for you. Keep meditating to keep up your happiness levels.

As a spiritual but not overly religious person, I am in awe when I sit down to a meal with my Christian friends and they say the blessing before a meal. In Catholicism you have a set of prayers, which even after all these years I can recite from memory – they are that drilled into you. However, these blessings are so beautiful and thoughtful that it often leaves me feeling inadequate in the praying department. I was too embarrassed to even voice these insecurities. I wished I could pray like my friends did. One day, while listening to a CD by the late and very great Dr. Wayne Dyer, he put my fears and insecurities to rest. I'm paraphrasing but he said simply "If you don't know how to pray, the most powerful prayer in the world is Thank You."

Feeling grateful and acknowledging all the good things in our lives is a great way to increase our overall happiness. Getting in the habit of showing and experiencing more gratitude is one of the most powerful ways to increase your feeling of happiness.

While it's all good and well to resolve to feel more gratitude and become happier, putting it into action is a little easier said than done. Thankfully, there's a simple little tool that will help you stay on track – a journal. A gratitude journal is a wonderful thing and something that can have a surprisingly big impact on your life. Best of all, you don't need anything fancy. Grab a pen and a notebook, or boot up your laptop or computer and open a word document. I've even included a gratitude section in the Happiness Journal in the back of this book to get you started.

Not only will your writing help you right away, as you compose each daily entry, you're also creating a great memento of your gratitude and happiness journey. Pull out your journal, curl up on the couch and read through it whenever you need a little boost of happiness. Seeing, in black and white, how far you've come throughout the past weeks, months and even years is truly amazing.

As you start to read about the events and people you felt grateful for in the past, you start to relive those memories, and with it those feelings. Think of your gratitude journal as a happiness battery. You're storing up good feelings in an easy format that allows you to access and relive them on demand. What a powerful idea.

In addition, writing and reading your gratitude journal regularly will help you form new positive habits. You'll start to have a more positive outlook on life, and since the journal forces you to think of and find the things and people you're grateful for in any given day, your brain will automatically start to look for the positive instead of the negative. It's easy to see how that can have a beneficial impact on your life over time. I encourage you to get started writing in your gratitude journal!

Another amazing phenomenon that begins to happen when you start practicing gratitude is that you immediately want to start giving back. I think back to when I was a kid, and how I couldn't wait for Christmas. It was all about the presents that I would GET. I'd spend days and weeks anticipating and trying to guess what Mom and Dad would get me this year. I'd make lists and circle things in toy catalogs. It was all about receiving material things.

As I've grown older, that has changed a bit. Don't get me wrong, I still appreciate a thoughtful gift, but to be honest, most of the fun at Christmas for me now is GIVING gifts. I find joy in the process of finding just the right gift, putting it in a pretty wrapper, and then seeing the eyes of the recipient light up when they open their present. And, of course, there is nothing more fun than watching little ones squeal with delight on Christmas morning as they open the gifts under the tree.

There's an important lesson to be learned here and that giving makes us happier. It isn't just about physical gifts. Anytime we can give something, be it our time, a kind word, sound advice, or a hug, it makes us feel good to give back. Giving – without a doubt – increases our own happiness. I had a boss once who told me that whenever he was feeling down, he would take his two little kids and they would go to Toys R Us. He said he would get a cart and he and the kids would fill it with all kinds of games and toys and puzzles etc. Then, he and the kids would take those bags and bags of fun and bring them to the Children's Wing of their local hospital. After hearing that story, it inspired me to give when I am feeling most down.

One time, a few years ago, I was working on a Naval Base in San Diego. I took a job just to have a job. Although it was a great experience, but not the most fulfilling job I've had and since I had just come from having my own business – it was sad as well. If the lack of satisfaction wasn't bad enough, the money was...bad. Money was really tight for me in San Diego – a place where you really need quite a bit of it. So – I was not feeling my happiest.

One day, I drove onto the base at the usual hour of 5:00am. I normally stopped at Starbucks on the base and got a coffee for myself rather than drink the swill the Navy calls coffee. On this day, I also decided to get a coffee for my co-worker, Cindy. I paid for those coffees with my Starbucks card, but when I went in my wallet to get it, I saw the final $20 bill I had to last me until pay day – 3 days away. I took the $20 out and handed it to the cashier. I asked her to use it to buy some enlisted sailors coffee that morning. She gladly accepted it and said she would do that. She thanked me for them. I had the very best day that day – nothing changed in my routine, but I was just happier. It was $20 well spent! I continue to look for opportunities to do similar things.

My friend Lynda is very funny – she has taken this Random Act of Kindness to a whole new level. Beginning on her 50th birthday, she decided that she would spend that day doing 50 random acts of kindness. She does everything from bringing in the neighbor's trash pails, putting money in meters, taping quarters to vending machines – you name it. Every year, she increases her acts of kindness by the birthday. What a great way to spend your birthday!

So, if you think receiving is great (and it is!) – giving is even greater. You will be amazed at how much happier you become with each act of kindness that you bestow on another.

Imagine if you will a little baby. The baby is born and put in a crib. It's not spoken to or held. As the baby grows, they move it to a larger crib, but no one is there to teach the baby how to walk or talk or eat or even what their name is. What kind of existence will that child have?

I'll repeat the quote I mentioned earlier – If you're not growing, you're dying. But, if you're not growing, you're also not growing happier. I have a friend who was born and raised in the same house. She met her first boyfriend and they got married. They moved within walking distance of her childhood home to an apartment. They went on their honeymoon. It was her first (and remains the only) airplane trip. They eventually bought a house, but only after her siblings did so – they moved close to them and also moved their parents.

They still live in the same house – 10 years later. They rent the same house on the same beach for the same two weeks every summer. They never go anywhere. They don't even go to the movies. They are the most miserable people I know. The find fault in everything. They often make fun of me because I could not be more opposite of them. I have moved cross-country twice. I have lived in many different apartments and cities. I travel whenever and wherever I get the chance. Even though I love my travel destinations, I try not to go to the same place twice because I love to try new things.

New experiences, new places, new people add so much to our lives. Could you imagine if you knew only the things you knew in high school – today?! Just keeping up with the speed of technology keeps us on our toes. My dad is a perfect example. I will cut him some slack, because he is 92 years old after all. He does have a cell phone – so kudos to him…but it's still a flip phone! Has no interest in a smartphone, and if he could get LESS technology on his phone he would love it. He does not text or IM or Facetime. He can barely retrieve a voicemail message! He finally let me teach him how to use the DVD player and the DVR recorder on the cable box (that took quite a bit of teaching!) He spends most of his days watching movies. Although he has quite a collection of DVDs – he has watched them all multiple, multiple times. I have subscriptions to both Netflix and Amazon Prime, but he has no interest in learning how to work the computer to watch them online.

How many new horizons are out there waiting for us to find them, explore them and let them enrich our lives – I can tell you there are as many as you are willing to try for….meaning there is no end to the personal growth you can achieve. Learning new things is such a confidence booster – and we know that confidence is a key component in happiness.

So what can you do to learn and grow? Well, I'm not suggesting that you enroll in college and get a degree or two – but if that is something you've always wanted to do – go for it. You can NEVER be too educated. Also, there are so many options for online schools these days, that it takes all the inconvenience out of dragging yourself there two to three nights each week, during times that might interfere with your day job. If higher education is for you, you would be well-served to pursue it.

However, maybe you already have your degree or are not interested in getting one – there are other ways to grow as well. What about travel to a foreign land? Italy? Greece? Israel? Those places are full of ancient history and culture. I've heard it said that no matter how much money you spend on travel, you always come back richer – because the experience alone is so rewarding.

If the funds for travel aren't in your bank account yet, perhaps you can start with learning the language of the place you want to visit. There are apps that you can get for your phone that can teach you another language. They're either free or pretty darn cheap. You also can't go wrong with learning another language. I read that the United States is the ONLY country where the majority of people speak only one language. It seems we get upset when people come to the United States and don't speak English, but we also get upset when we travel OUT of the US and find that people don't speak English – even though they are in their native country. Get with the program and learn another language (full disclosure – I only speak English – but learning French is on my list!)

What about a craft or hobby? Is there anything you ever wanted to learn how to do? I marvel at my friends who can knit and crochet. I have tried to knit and it was a laughable experience. I managed to learn how to crochet (two stitches). Those two stitches allowed me to make baby blankets and afghans. So I made them by the dozens! I made them for everyone I knew having a baby (I still do!) and I made afghans for all my friends to match the décor in their homes. I would make additional afghans with all my leftover yarn and at Christmas time I would bring the blankets to a nursing home with a tray of cookies for them to distribute as they see fit among the residents. Kind of like killing two birds with one stone – I learn something new, make something pretty and give it away.

Something else to consider is volunteering. There are so many opportunities that don't take a lot of time or commitment. As I write this, my Dad is in the hospital. I'm sitting in his room with him and the volunteers come around and refill his water jug or just to come in and say "hi". It's very sweet. When my Dad's companion was in a nursing home before she passed away, a young woman would come in once a week and polish her nails. You could spend a weekend – or a week volunteering for a Habitat for Humanity project. That would be an awesome thing to do – especially if you own, or are considering owning your own home. I bet you would pick up some mad skills doing that. They even have Habitat for Humanity projects that are for women only. How cool would that be?

If none of the above appeals to you – I can suggest my fail safe. Something I turn to every night. A book. A good old fashioned book. You can download them on your devices – I do that too, but I really love the look, feel and smell of a book. These days I read mostly educational books – I am always trying to pick up some new skills – whether it be coaching skills, or something technical that will help me with my website. But every now and then, I just love to pick up a fiction book…mysteries in particular. It doesn't really matter what you read, you will learn something from any book. A book is an adventure you can hold in your hands…and they are cheap too – or free…just check your local library.

Expanding your brain, expanding your horizons also expands your happiness levels…don't believe me? I dare you to try it!!!

CHAPTER NINE

Career

What do you want to be when you grow up? How many times were you asked that question when you were a kid? How many answers did you give over the years? I remember briefly wanting to be a doctor or a nurse – until I found out that you had to dissect things in school. For the longest time after that, I wanted to be a lawyer – yet I ended up doing none of that and landed on Wall Street.

Every day I hear stories of people who feel that they are at a crossroads in their lives. They aren't satisfied with their careers and some wonder how you got there in the first place. How you got there is the easy question to answer. How many little boys (or girls) do you know that wanted to be firemen when they grew up? It's so cute when they're little. The parents or relatives and friends buys them the helmet a little fire truck and encourage them. But, as they grow older, if they still hold that dream, what often happens is that they are gently guided or influenced by their parents into a different, safer career.

This isn't malicious or ill willed on the parent's part, they only want what is best for their child to keep them safe. Or, in the case of an acquaintance of mine who aspired to go into show business. She wanted to be an actress. She was quite a performer – she could sing, dance and act. Her parents "indulged" her aspirations during middle school and most of high school, but as she prepared to go to college, they "gently" persuaded her to seek a "practical" degree. She is now a successful business owner in the technology sector but is struggling because it is not her passion and now it is coming to light. When the feelings first started to surface, she talked to her mother about it. She asked her why she didn't encourage her to pursue acting as a career. Her mother explained that she knew what a cut throat and cruel world Hollywood can be – especially to women, and she wanted to spare her beautiful daughter that at all costs. Our futures are often shaped by well-meaning people who, although they have our best interests at heart are shaped by their own views, opinions and insecurities.

Maybe this isn't you – maybe your parents were 100% supportive of your dreams and aspirations and they cheered and supported you at every turn. You want to be a circus performer? Great – they buy stock in peanuts. You want to be a veterinarian – even though you are allergic to cats AND dogs? They're right behind you with the Benadryl and a box of tissues. An attorney? They've bought you every season DVD of Law and Order – and watch it with you! You are hell bent to achieve your dreams, but halfway through college you have a change of heart and have to face your parents. Or worse, you feel like you can't disappoint them, so you continue on with a course of study that you know isn't what you want to do.

Here's another scenario that often happens – you go to college and follow the course of study that you really believe is your passion. For the sake of argument, let's say it's fashion design. You graduate with good grades – maybe not at the top of your class but certainly respectable. Now you have to find work. Unfortunately that is not easy. It's a competitive marketplace and the best jobs are being scooped up by the honor roll students. You need to make money, because your student loans will be kicking in soon and you will have to repay them, so you take a job in a completely different field – insurance sales. You say you'll only do this for a year, to make some money, all the while continuing to look for work in your field of choice. Turns out though, that you're pretty good at the insurance thing. You're making really good money and you're living well. You postpone finding your passion in lieu of the comfortable.

While it appears that everything is going well for you, it's only a bandage over a blistering wound. You know this isn't right, but... Outwardly, everyone is cheering you on and so proud, but inside – something is brewing – and it is only a matter of time before it boils over. Some folks realize it at 25 years old or 30…but more and more I see people at 40, 50 and 60 that are now just becoming brave enough to stop and completely change course.

What I would like, more than anything else, for you to get from this chapter is that whatever you're feeling about your career – is okay. Seriously, how are you supposed to know what you want to do for the rest of your life when you are 18 years old? Would you take career advice from a high school kid? I would bet my last dollar that you would not! What I would like is for you to examine what it is you want to be/should be doing and make a plan to start doing that. Only by being true to ourselves can we be truly happy.

The thing that stops most people from taking that leap is that they are very conscious of the appearance of it to others. What will my parents think, if I suddenly renounce my career as a successful attorney to become a nightclub singer? What will my boss think when I resign and tell him I am leaving my executive position at his insurance company to become a cowboy in the rodeo? These examples are designed to make you laugh but to also point out that nothing is off limits.

I will let you in on a little secret that has not only helped me immensely, but has also changed my life. If you know anything about me at all, you know how I adore Dr. Wayne Dyer. Well, I listened to him when he laid this pearl of wisdom on me…"what other people think of you is none of your business." Wow. What?

It's true, though. Other people's opinions of you (good or bad) are colored by their own life experiences and perceptions. I'll give you two quick examples to illustrate my point. My cousin Judy thinks I walk on water. She's called me a saint, and she doesn't think there is anything I couldn't do. I really believe that she thinks I could be the Queen of England. By contrast, this guy I used to work with, Kenny, came up to me and said "I want to tell you a joke – it's a dumb blonde joke – no offense."

What would happen if I took their opinions of me to heart? How would I act if I believed I was the Queen of England...I think probably that I would be expecting people to wait on me hand and foot. If I was truly a dumb blonde (I am neither!) I might not have the confidence in my abilities to succeed at anything. I say this to impress upon you that the opinion of others is just that...their opinion. And it has absolutely nothing to do with you or your abilities.

So, how you got to where you are is no longer a mystery. It's nobody's fault that you are where you are, and you are where you are because it's exactly where you are supposed to be right now. Where you go from here is up to you, and this might be where the real work comes in for you... because you may not even KNOW what it is that you want to do with your life. While being a cowboy was your childhood dream, you might not feel the same way as a 38 year old man. The trick is to find a way to make a living that makes you actually feel alive and ignites your passion.

Great, you say, but exactly how do I do that?! Obviously, the answer will be different for everyone, but start where it feels good. What do you LIKE to do? Is there something that you would do even if you didn't get paid for it? If there is, that's what you should be doing! You might not even need to quit your day job!

Say you love to bake, spend your off time working on perfecting whatever it is you like to bake. Find that perfect chocolate chip cookie recipe or design your own. Make a killer apple pie, or cupcakes to die for…then pack up those bad boys and bring them to your place of employment. The first thing that happens is that you become VERY popular at your job. People begin stopping by your desk…just to see if there are any new goodies around…but these people are also your prospective customers. You bring in those beautiful pink cupcakes and the next thing you know, Sally from accounting is asking you to bake some for her daughter's birthday party. You'll get a taste of what it might be like to be in the cupcake business and decide if it's something you'd like to take further. You might just find that you don't need to change careers, that baking for your friends and co-workers is fulfilling to you. You can be available for baking for others on a case by case basis and not have to commit to starting your own business or change careers.

If you love to act, you might be able to get your fix by joining a local theater company. Like to read? Put an ad out on fiverr.com or freelancer.com for some editing gigs…you get to read new material and make some money on the side. The beauty of trying to "find yourself" when you're older is that you have more life experience and you are usually able to determine more quickly whether this is something that you want to do as a career.

Some folks, myself included, had fears that they were too old to "start again." Last year, shortly after I turned 57 years old and was just beginning my coaching practice, I had second thoughts and some doubts about being too old to start something new. I was really concerned about my age, until a friend sent me something he found on Facebook that pointed out that at 57 years old, Colonel Sanders was living in his car. Self-help guru Louise Hay was bouncing checks, and at 57 years old, authors Laura Ingalls Wilder (Little House on the Prairie) and Stephen Covey (The 7 Habits of Highly Effective People) had yet to publish one book.

Age is really just number. There is no limit to what you can accomplish no matter what your age. In fact, there are many professions, including coaching that tend to benefit from age and experience. If you were a 50 year old, would you look for a life coach who was 25 years old? Probably not – while they may have gotten training and even become certified, there is a certain security in sharing your story with someone that has actually experienced life. At 25, most folks have not really had that opportunity or experience.

Don't celebrate your age on your birthdays, celebrate your experience. Today, I have 50, 60, 67, 75 85 years of experience – now bring me some cake!

CHAPTER TEN

Money

If I had to divide my clients by the topics of which they sought coaching for, money would be in the top three...along with love and weight. Mind you, they don't start out telling me that's what they want, it's usually couched in the "I just want to be happy" category, but when we drill down, money usually rears its ugly head (or, as we will come to view it – its most beautiful head!). My clients either don't make enough money, have too much debt, or both. I'll cover as much as I can in this chapter, to hopefully give you a handle on both as it pertains to your happiness. I'm going to narrow it to saving, debt and income.

Saving – If you get only one message from this chapter it would be to start saving for your retirement...NOW. It's never too early to start saving, and on the other hand – it's never too late to save either. You can believe me when I tell you this is from experience. During my career I have worked for many prestigious firms, all of whom offered a savings or 401(k) plan for retirement. I always told myself that I was too young to think about retirement (I was in my 20's for goodness sake!) or that I couldn't afford it.

Needless to say, as I near retirement age, I don't have near enough money saved as I would like. Luckily, the work I do does not feel like work, so retirement doesn't feel imminent. However, at some point you may want to step away from the workforce. Having financial resources will make that a heck of alot easier.

So, my advice for this section would be to start. Just start. If you are fortunate enough to work for an employer that offers a 401 (k) or similar plan for your retirement – you should sign up for it immediately. At the beginning, I don't care if you have them deduct just $5 from your pay. Start somewhere. That said, if your employer offers any kind of matching funds, I would do everything in my power to reach the point where you are getting every penny your employer will match. My research shows that many employers offer a match of 50% to your 6% - so if you save 6% of your salary, they will contribute an additional 3%. Why wouldn't you do that? It's like saying no to free money!

I already know your first argument. "But I can't afford to have any less money in my paycheck...I need every penny." Trust me when I tell you that you can't afford NOT to do this. When you're in your 20's, retirement seems far away. It comes up on you quick. You can also trust me when I tell you that retirement is very costly! Social Security, if it's still around when you retire, will not come near covering your expenses. You will need additional income, so unless you want to be a Walmart greeter at 98 years old, you better start putting some money away.

Chances are you will not even feel the deduction – especially if you start small. The money comes out of your salary pre-tax, so you pay less tax on the cash. What ends up in your paycheck might be pretty close to what you were already getting. What I'd also like you to look at at this time is your Federal withholding. If you wait all year for a huge tax refund in the spring, you are having too much money withheld from your pay. Getting a big refund is great, but not at the expense of your day to day living. Why would you let the government use your money interest free? They certainly won't do that for you. Consider upping your withholding... but don't do it too much...you don't want to end up owing the IRS either

– those people do NOT have a sense of humor! Doing this may find enough money for you to make your savings plan!

I would also increase my savings by half of whatever my raise was that year. So, if I received a merit increase of 5%, I would increase my 401 (k) savings by 2 or 3%. I was saving more, but also keeping some…win/win. When you start to see your retirement savings grow, you will get excited and be motivated to see it grow bigger and bigger.

You will also need to start a regular savings account – for unexpected expenses, or a vacation or a new car…The good news with this savings is that it is completely liquid and easily accessible, so if you hit a tough week and you need it for groceries you can tap into it. But try not to do that! I have some fun games that I play with myself to trick me into saving money. Maybe one (or all) will work for you.

As with your 401 (k) savings, if you can have some of salary automatically deposited in your savings account, you should do that – even if it's just five dollars. If you don't see it, you can't spend it. When your next paycheck rolls around, if there is any money left in your checking account, throw that into your savings…You can also set up (if your bank offers it) one of those "keep the change" actions…so if you spend $2.10 at Starbucks, they will round up your spend and roll the $.90 into savings – that adds up quickly. Two more little tricks…every time I work out at the gym I throw a dollar into a jar I keep in my bedroom. When the jar is full, I take that to the bank and put it right into my savings. Finally, I do one of those progressive saves that I found on Pinterest…on week one you save one dollar, on week two you save two dollars and so on and so forth. At the end of 52 weeks, you will have save in excess of $1300. The one I did started in January, so it had me saving the most money at the end of the year – when I am usually spending money on Christmas etc…so I did mine in reverse. I started my week one saving $52, and week two saving $51…so by the end of the year, I was saving $5, $4, $3 etc…Saving money then becomes fun and not something to be dreaded.

DEBT

No doubt about it, debt sucks. I hate it but sometimes it's a necessary evil. I'm not talking about a mortgage here or even student loans. I'm talking mainly about personal loans, revolving lines of credit, and credit cards. I've seen it happen in my own life and countless others. You can get credit card offers in the mail or at the store. You take advantage of it because it's a good deal at the time, and you think you'll pay in full when the bill comes in. Maybe you do. Maybe that happens for a couple of months and then for some reason or another you only pay the minimum, and then that gets comfortable and then you're only paying the minimum on a growing balance. Before you know it, the minimum is all you can pay and there's no money left to live on so now you're living on credit. It's a vicious cycle. Then, if you're like me, I was in denial of what I owed. I never even look at the balances on my statements. Sometimes I would get so overwhelmed that I just didn't pay them at all, which created more problems. So if this sounds familiar it's because I've been there and I can empathize with you.

You can fix it though. The first step is to be brave. Get the latest statements from all of your accounts and sit down with the calculator and figure out what you owe. Just get the number. It might be scary and it may make you want to throw up when you see it but it gets better from here – I promise. If you are behind on any accounts you may want to call your creditors to see if they will make arrangements with you. I will save you a little time by telling you that unless you are behind a few late or missed payments they are less likely to work with you. They will play hardball and hold your credit rating over your head. However, when you're very late they are more apt to work with you and get something from you rather than expecting that you might stiff them altogether.

Let's assume though that you have all your numbers and you don't have to contact anyone. You just want to pay off the debt. Most "experts" will tell you to start with the account that has the highest interest and pay the most on that each month until it is paid off. This makes sense financially, but money isn't always about the dollars and cents. There's a psychological piece to it too, and this chapter is about your happiness and your money – it's about what makes sense as opposed to the cents of it all. So I lineup all my bills and I make minimum payments on all of them with the exception of the account with the smallest balance. I throw the balance of my bill paying money on that account and pay that off as soon as possible. When that account is paid off, you take a big ole red magic marker and write PAID IN FULL all over that sucker! You keep it in the file with your other bills so that you can see it during bill paying time. Then, you move on to the next smallest balance and get to work on that. Which do you think will make you feel better…say you have 5 accounts. The smallest one has a balance of $500, and it's also the lowest interest rate. Your largest account has a balance of $10,000 and it has the highest interest rate. Logically, you would pay down the account with the highest rate. But with that $10,000 balance, it's going to take you quite a while to pay it off. Meanwhile, all those other accounts are there as well – you feel like you're not making a dent in anything. When you see that PAID IN FULL when you pull out your bill folder, you will get so motivated to pay the others. Try it…I think you will find tremendous satisfaction in doing so.

Paying off the smaller accounts also has other benefits. It's also one less account to keep track of, one less thing to stress over. It wasn't too long ago I had a lot of credit card accounts. I had bought a condo and needed everything, so everywhere shopped I opened an account. It wasn't a matter of the money, I had enough to pay the bills, but it was the fact that it was like 15 accounts that I had to keep track of. I pay them online so it was 15 logons, 15 passwords, 15 payable dates, and on and on. Because nothing sucks your bank account like a new house, I was carrying balances on all of those cards. While it wasn't a problem at the time, I knew if I kept up that pace of spending it would cause problems. So I sat down for couple of hours and devised my plan to pay off my debt.

The first thing I noticed was that I had spent a lot more than I thought I had. Credit cards are both a lifesaver and the devil. They certainly come in handy when you need something and don't have the cash, but when you're shopping with plastic and those green bills are not coming out of your wallet right then and there we tend to spend more. The other thing I noticed was how much interest I was paying. When you see $20 in interest charge that month, it doesn't seem SO bad, but when you look at the total year to date and realize that was a car payment - or CAR - it's a bit of a shock! I set up a schedule to pay my bills twice per month. I divide them into two categories – the First of the Month and the Fifteenth of the month. I pay all of my household bills – regardless of their payable date on the first of the month – mortgage, homeowners association, gas, electric, cable and cell phone. On the fifteenth, I pay all credit cards, car payment etc. Each pay "cycle" includes savings and other expenses like food and gas and entertainment.

Most of the unhappiness that surrounds debt is due to lack of control. Getting a system in place to pay off your debt gives you back control. Knowing what you owe gives you power and helps you control your spending as well. If you know you're $30,000 in debt, chances are you are going to pass by that cute jacket or set of golf clubs. Paying off those cards and writing PAID IN FULL will boost your confidence more than that jacket ever will! When I did this, I felt so in control, that I not only paid the account in full, but I called the creditor and asked them to CLOSE my account. I still keep a couple of cards available that I use for rewards or cash back, but now I don't spend what I can't pay for in cash, and I don't even wait for the bill to come in, I pay it off as soon as the charge hits the account..

This is a process, and paying down debt does not happen overnight – unless you win the lottery. However, taking the first step, and getting control WILL increase your happiness as it pertains to your debt.

BUYING VS. RENTING

As I write this I'm 58 years old and I bought my first residence, a condo, two years ago. Until I purchased my own place, I never had any interest in buying. I thought it too restrictive, too binding. I can't get up and move whenever the mood strikes me. I also thought I would need a lot more money for a down payment and could never imagine accumulating the money needed for down payment. As a single woman living alone, there was a certain comfort in living in apartments where if something broke it was usually someone else's responsibility to fix it. However, two years ago I was kind of forced into buying. I had been renting a two-story town-home when my dad moved in with me. All the bedrooms were upstairs and there was only a half bath on the main floor. It soon became impossible for him to make the stairs, and it was clear I would need to find another place to live. Of course I looked at rentals first. I wasn't even considering owning. However, I now had a strict criteria that I needed to meet due to my dad's physical limitations. Add to that a lack of housing here in this booming location and the rising (astronomically) cost of renting and you can see how my arm was twisted into looking into ownership. I was scared to death when someone mentioned buying my own place.

I never even thought I would get approved for the mortgage and was concerned about my lack of a healthy down payment, but I firmly believe that when something is supposed to happen for you nothing can stop it. From the day I first considered buying until I closed on the mortgage and was handed the keys, only 63 days had passed. Crazy! Now, after owning for two years, I could kick myself for not having done it sooner. When I think of all the rent I have paid over the last 30 years it's like burning that money in the backyard or throwing it out the window. Add to that all the tax write offs I missed out on and that's more money wasted.

But there's more. As with paying off the credit cards and starting your retirement savings there is a certain confidence factor in owning your own home. it just feels so grown-up. It doesn't have anything to do with the mortgage; I've spent more on rent than I am currently paying on my mortgage it's like you were seen as more responsible. I have such pride in owning my condo. I take good care of it and I also make it a point to know my neighbors and keep an eye out for a whole property, so I guess I'm a better -maybe not better - but a more active citizen. Every dollar you spend on your mortgage is building equity for your future. When you rent you're paying towards someone else's future.

INCOME

So saving money and paying your debts is a lot easier when you're actually making enough money to live on. We talk about what you do to actually make your money in our career section, so if you're skipping around in the chapters, please go check that out…but let's assume for the sake of this chapter that your job doesn't suck but you just need more money.

I have always felt that if I come right out and ask for something it's usually given to me. I don't just ask and expect to receive without giving something in return, but I always plan my conversation and expect it to go my way. When I was an hourly worker, I have gone to my bosses and explained that I needed more money…were there additional shifts I could work? I would make sure that I was available for the shifts that I knew others didn't want to work and usually got those hours.

When I became a salaried worker and my pay wasn't cutting it, I would go to my boss and ask – what do I need to do to earn more money? I would be ready to tell him how much money I needed to earn when he asked. I have always been an exemplary employee. I go above and beyond for any boss that I have ever had (even the terrible ones!) and then, when I need it – it pays off. I have never gone to a boss and asked for additional money and been turned down. Never. The thing is – if you don't ask, the answer is always NO…

If you have some extra hours at the end of your week, perhaps you can get yourself a side gig. I've worked at Toys R Us during the holiday (don't do that!) and held other side jobs...I once took a side job in the shoe department of Lord and Taylor – thank goodness I did it just to kill time over a bad break up and not to make money...because I didn't bring home ONE RED CENT! I spent every single dollar (and more!) that I had made during that time. Uber and Lyft are great for earning some extra cash in your spare time as well.

If you can't work at a brick and mortar building because you need to be at home, but you have some technical skills, you can pick up gigs on sites like fiverr.com and freelancer.com. Do you have a hobby that you like to do in your spare time that can make you some money? My friend likes to sew. She started out making aprons for her sisters and when her friends saw them they wanted them...one thing led to another, and now she is about to open her own store on Etsy...who would have thought aprons were in such demand?

The thing is that the money you need – in whatever quantity you need is already here for you. Your getting rich doesn't make someone else poor. There is an endless supply of money and resources out there. You need to decide what you need and why you need it and then the ideas will start to come to you and the Universe will move you into the path of making it happen. This has happened in my own life and I have seen it happen in the lives of the people that I have and am coaching.

In the career chapter I talk about owning your own business. If starting a traditional business does not appeal to you, maybe you would consider a network marketing business. I know, I know – you hate those people! The truth of the matter is that network marketing is one of the greatest vehicles you can use to generate income for yourself...and if you do it right, for your children!

The first thing a network marketing business does for you is gives you a tax status as a business owner, which, right off the bat will save you money on your taxes. There are a whole bunch (technical term) of deductions you can claim as a business owner. The next thing it does – and the biggest benefit network marketing brings to you is that it gives you the ability to stop trading your time for money. In a traditional job, you go to work and trade 40 hours for however much money they pay you. If you have a consulting business or you sell something, you trade your time and are compensated by what you sell. Need more money, you have to find more clients or sell more widgets.

When you have a network marketing business, you make money on the work that other people are doing…residual income. You're not trading time for dollars any more. As your downline works to make themselves money, they are making money for you too. People claim that network marketing is a pyramid scheme – that no one makes money except the guys at the top…when you think of it though, regular businesses are the pyramid schemes…who makes the most money in a traditional business? The President or the CEO, right? Does Joe in accounting have any opportunity for doing that? Probably not, but in network marketing he does. Another complaint I hear is that people hate it when their friends prospect them. I don't know about you, but I actually like buying from my friends. If I am looking for a specific good or service, I will most always reach out to my friends and family first for a recommendation. If I personally knew of someone selling something that I needed, I wouldn't hesitate to seek them out first. I would shop with them every chance I got.

Another complaint I hear regarding network marketing companies is about recruiting – they feel like their friends are trying to get them to sign up and work the business. We live in America, and the last time I looked anyway, we still had free will. I am reminded of this (very sad) story about September 11, 2001. Wall Street firm Cantor Fitzgerald was headquartered on the 101st-105th floors of One World Trade Center. Everyone in the office that morning perished, and the only ones to survive were the people that were not at work that day for some fluke one off reason…CEO Howard

Lutnick was taking his child to their first day of school. Someone else missed the train, another, had stepped outside to make a coffee run. Why am I telling this particular story? Well, during the aftermath of that horrific event, I remember a news piece being done about the Cantor Fitzgerald employees that were in the West Coast office watching this thing unfold. One person said that she could no longer look at her wedding photos, because her whole bridal party was made up of friends and family who all worked at Cantor.

They went on to say how the firm was such a great place to work that they would always recommend a friend or a family member if a position became available. If my friend or family member thought enough of me to refer me to their employer and thought enough of their employer to refer them to me, I would be flattered – not pissed off or offended. If the company or the job wasn't a fit for me, I am always free to say so – and so are you if someone offers you an opportunity to partner with them in a network marketing venture. But how cool would it be, to find a product or service that you really use and believe in, and to make a career out of it (or some side moolah) and do it having fun with my friends and family? Sounds pretty sweet if you ask me!

Network money isn't easy money – but it can be fun and rewarding... especially if you are working with friends. It's also a very affordable and low risk way to get into your own business. I urge you to, if not give it a go, to at least keep yourself open to the possibility. If you haven't ever considered it before, it might be a good time to check them out. I don't have ties to any of these companies, but a couple that I like and would recommend you look at are – Nu Skin, Isagenix and Rodan & Fields.

CHAPTER ELEVEN

Habits

So we talked about all these things, and you've gotten some ideas that you would like to implement in your life to bring you more happiness…but how do you maintain it? You have to create a habit. As I mentioned in the beginning, not only is happiness a choice, but it is a habit. You may be one of those people that has to make a conscious decision each day to be happy. Once you decide to be happy, then you have to act on it. If you wake up in the morning and say "today, I'm going to be happy" and then turn over, pull the covers over your head and stay in bed all day – that is not going to help you.

If you want to be a happy person, start the habit of being happy. I have a saying that I use all the time and it is – "fake it till you make it." You usually hear it in the business and show business world, but you can use it in your life too. The idea is that if you look like a success, others around you will treat you like a successful person and will send more projects and opportunities your way. At some point, the idea is that you can stop faking it because you've become what you've pretended to be. It sounds a little harsher than it is. Faking in this context isn't as phony as it sounds. What you are really doing is modeling behaviors until you've internalized them. Once that happens, you will start to see results, because you've been working hard at exactly the types of things a successful person does. It only makes sense then that you start to see results.

The interesting thing is that this works in all sorts of different contexts. If you want to be a thin and fit person, start acting like one, eating the things they eat, working out, moving around more etc. After a few months of doing that, it's no wonder that you're starting to slim down.

Since happiness is on my mind a lot during this project, I did a little research to see if the same concept could also work for feelings – including increasing a feeling of self-worth, well-being and of course, being happier. The good news is that it does. You really can fake happiness until your mood improves. Doing so is a lot easier than you may think. You can start with nothing more complicated than smiling. A fake smile will do in a pinch, but if you can, try getting your entire face, including your eyes, involved. Give smiling your best effort, even if you aren't feeling it.

After a bit of smiling, you should feel your mood start to improve. Remind yourself throughout the day to smile more for best results. When you're ready to kick it up a notch, give laughing out loud a try. Again, if there's nothing funny going on, just start giggling and laughing. It has a profound effect on your body. Plus, if you're not alone, the looks people start to give you when you are laughing at nothing will really give you something to laugh about! Not only does laughing instantly lift your bad mood, but as I mentioned earlier, it has also been shown to increase your body's ability to heal itself and it will improve your immune system.

If you need to, you can start by faking it, but creating a habit of happiness takes consistency. I have found that the best way to be consistent is to track the activity or habit that I am trying to develop. If I'm trying to save money, I might journal all of my expenses for a month to determine where I spend all my money. We've all been told to journal our food intake when we are trying to shed some pounds. If you're trying to beef up your workout routine, you might keep a journal of what you did in the gym or how much you walked or ran each day. Keeping a journal not only reminds you to complete your tasks, but it also is a record of how far you've come.

They say that it takes 21 days to start a new habit. In my experience, I believe it takes a bit longer, say 45 days. I've split the difference and included a happiness journal for you on the following pages that I hope will give you a head start on creating your own happiness habit. It's a guided journal, with just a few simple questions for you to answer each day. At the end of each day ask yourself the questions and write down your answers and don't forget to include any thoughts you might have concerning your quest to happiness. As you move through the next 31 days, you'll be able to record your thoughts and progress as you make the choice to be happy and making happiness a focal point of your life.

Here are a few other fun things to help you on your way:

1. Write the word HAPPY in large letters on a sheet of paper and put it where you'll see it upon waking every morning – like the bathroom mirror. Each day, when you see that note, make the conscious decision to be happy.

2. Check yourself during the day. Maybe you can make another note and stick it inside your notebook – so that when you open the notebook you see the word HAPPY. Another idea is to put it in your online calendar like an appointment – when the reminder pops up telling you that you have an appointment to Go Happy Yourself!!

3. Make a choice to be happy no matter what happens to you each day.

4. Meditate or pray about your circumstances and how you can be happy because of, or in spite of them.

5. Buddy up! It's always more fun to do things in pairs. Ask a friend to join you in your happiness quest. Be happiness accountability partners.

I really hope that you have enjoyed this book. My goal was to present you with some humor, and some interesting concepts that make you think and look at happiness in a different light. Most importantly, I want you to realize that happiness is within your grasp. It's up to you to make the right choices to increase your own happiness. Remember that it isn't about accumulating more things or wealth, and it isn't about improving your circumstances. The main way you can take control of your happiness is by changing the way you look at it and the world around you. Happiness is an attitude and it's one that you can start and strengthen…it all starts with a smile.

We've covered a lot of topics in this book, from the scientific data into happiness and why your happiness matters, to the different areas in our lives where happiness is paramount. The most important lesson that I want you to take away from reading this is that happiness is a choice and it is yours to make. You have control over it and you can do a lot to feel happier no matter what your circumstances are. That in itself is an amazing feeling. You are in control. What do you choose? I sincerely hope you choose to Go Happy Yourself!!

Your **31-Day** Journal

DAY 1

DATE: _ _ _ _ _ _ _ _ _ _

Circle the appropriate answer:

Was I happy today?	Y/N
Did I eat nutritiously?	Y/N
Did I exercise today?	Y/N
Did I sleep well last night?	Y/N
Did I meditate today?	Y/N
Did I take time for myself today?	Y/N

» What am I grateful for today?

_____

_____

_____

_____

» How did I CHOOSE to be happy today?

_____

_____

_____

_____

» How did my happiness or lack of happiness affect others today?

_____

_____

_____

_____

» What more could I have done to be happy today?

_____

_____

_____

_____

Go Happy Yourself!! – Coach Jamie Lee

DAY 2

DATE: _ _ _ _ _ _ _ _ _ _

Circle the appropriate answer:

Was I happy today?	Y/N
Did I eat nutritiously?	Y/N
Did I exercise today?	Y/N
Did I sleep well last night?	Y/N
Did I meditate today?	Y/N
Did I take time for myself today?	Y/N

» What am I grateful for today?

_____

_____

_____

_____

» How did I CHOOSE to be happy today?

_____

_____

_____

_____

» How did my happiness or lack of happiness affect others today?

_____

_____

_____

_____

» What more could I have done to be happy today?

_____

_____

_____

_____

Happiness is the secret to all beauty. There is no beauty without happiness.
- Christian Dior

DAY 3

DATE: _ _ _ _ _ _ _ _ _ _

Circle the appropriate answer:

Was I happy today?	Y/N
Did I eat nutritiously?	Y/N
Did I exercise today?	Y/N
Did I sleep well last night?	Y/N
Did I meditate today?	Y/N
Did I take time for myself today?	Y/N

» What am I grateful for today?

_____

_____

_____

_____

» How did I CHOOSE to be happy today?

_____

_____

_____

_____

» How did my happiness or lack of happiness affect others today?

_____

_____

_____

_____

» What more could I have done to be happy today?

_____

_____

_____

_____

Happiness comes from within and is found in the present moment by making peace with the past and looking forward to the future.

DAY 4

DATE: _ _ _ _ _ _ _ _ _

Circle the appropriate answer:

Was I happy today?	Y/N
Did I eat nutritiously?	Y/N
Did I exercise today?	Y/N
Did I sleep well last night?	Y/N
Did I meditate today?	Y/N
Did I take time for myself today?	Y/N

» What am I grateful for today?

_____

_____

_____

_____

» How did I CHOOSE to be happy today?

_____

_____

_____

_____

» How did my happiness or lack of happiness affect others today?

_____

_____

_____

_____

» What more could I have done to be happy today?

_____

_____

_____

_____

*The key to happiness is letting each situation be what it is
instead of what you think it should be.*

DAY 5

DATE: _ _ _ _ _ _ _ _ _ _

Circle the appropriate answer:

Was I happy today?	Y/N
Did I eat nutritiously?	Y/N
Did I exercise today?	Y/N
Did I sleep well last night?	Y/N
Did I meditate today?	Y/N
Did I take time for myself today?	Y/N

» What am I grateful for today?

_____

_____

_____

_____

» How did I CHOOSE to be happy today?

_____

_____

_____

_____

» How did my happiness or lack of happiness affect others today?

_____

_____

_____

» What more could I have done to be happy today?

_____

_____

_____

The secret of being happy is accepting
where you are in life and making the most out of every day.

DAY 6

DATE: _ _ _ _ _ _ _ _ _

Circle the appropriate answer:

Was I happy today?	Y/N
Did I eat nutritiously?	Y/N
Did I exercise today?	Y/N
Did I sleep well last night?	Y/N
Did I meditate today?	Y/N
Did I take time for myself today?	Y/N

» What am I grateful for today?

_____

_____

_____

_____

» How did I CHOOSE to be happy today?

_____

_____

_____

_____

» How did my happiness or lack of happiness affect others today?

_____

_____

_____

_____

» What more could I have done to be happy today?

_____

_____

_____

_____

Happiness often sneaks in through a door
you didn't know you left open. - John Barrymore

DAY 7

DATE: _ _ _ _ _ _ _ _ _ _

Circle the appropriate answer:

Was I happy today?	Y/N
Did I eat nutritiously?	Y/N
Did I exercise today?	Y/N
Did I sleep well last night?	Y/N
Did I meditate today?	Y/N
Did I take time for myself today?	Y/N

» What am I grateful for today?

_____

_____

_____

_____

» How did I CHOOSE to be happy today?

_____

_____

_____

_____

» How did my happiness or lack of happiness affect others today?

_____

_____

_____

_____

» What more could I have done to be happy today?

_____

_____

_____

_____

Don't put the key to your happiness in someone else's pocket.

DAY 8

DATE: _ _ _ _ _ _ _ _ _ _

Circle the appropriate answer:

Was I happy today?	Y/N
Did I eat nutritiously?	Y/N
Did I exercise today?	Y/N
Did I sleep well last night?	Y/N
Did I meditate today?	Y/N
Did I take time for myself today?	Y/N

» What am I grateful for today?

_____

_____

_____

_____

» How did I CHOOSE to be happy today?

_____

_____

_____

_____

» How did my happiness or lack of happiness affect others today?

_____

_____

_____

_____

» What more could I have done to be happy today?

_____

_____

_____

_____

We tend to forget that happiness doesn't come as a result of getting something we don't have, but rather recognizing & appreciating what we do have - Frederick Koenig

DAY 9

DATE: _ _ _ _ _ _ _ _ _ _

Circle the appropriate answer:

Was I happy today?	Y/N
Did I eat nutritiously?	Y/N
Did I exercise today?	Y/N
Did I sleep well last night?	Y/N
Did I meditate today?	Y/N
Did I take time for myself today?	Y/N

» What am I grateful for today?

_____

_____

_____

_____

» How did I CHOOSE to be happy today?

_____

_____

_____

_____

» How did my happiness or lack of happiness affect others today?

_____

_____

_____

_____

» What more could I have done to be happy today?

_____

_____

_____

_____

Happiness is not a goal; it is a by-product. -Eleanor Roosevelt

DAY 10

DATE: _ _ _ _ _ _ _ _ _ _

Circle the appropriate answer:

Was I happy today?	Y/N
Did I eat nutritiously?	Y/N
Did I exercise today?	Y/N
Did I sleep well last night?	Y/N
Did I meditate today?	Y/N
Did I take time for myself today?	Y/N

» What am I grateful for today?

_____

_____

_____

_____

» How did I CHOOSE to be happy today?

_____

_____

_____

_____

» How did my happiness or lack of happiness affect others today?

_____

_____

_____

_____

» What more could I have done to be happy today?

_____

_____

_____

_____

For every minute you are angry you lose sixty seconds of happiness.

DAY 11

DATE: _ _ _ _ _ _ _ _ _ _

Circle the appropriate answer:

Was I happy today?	Y/N
Did I eat nutritiously?	Y/N
Did I exercise today?	Y/N
Did I sleep well last night?	Y/N
Did I meditate today?	Y/N
Did I take time for myself today?	Y/N

» What am I grateful for today?

_____

_____

_____

_____

» How did I CHOOSE to be happy today?

_____

_____

_____

_____

» How did my happiness or lack of happiness affect others today?

_____

_____

_____

_____

» What more could I have done to be happy today?

_____

_____

_____

_____

Happiness is not the absence of problems,
it's the ability to deal with them. - Steve Maraboli

DAY 12

DATE: _ _ _ _ _ _ _ _ _ _

Circle the appropriate answer:

Was I happy today?	Y/N
Did I eat nutritiously?	Y/N
Did I exercise today?	Y/N
Did I sleep well last night?	Y/N
Did I meditate today?	Y/N
Did I take time for myself today?	Y/N

» What am I grateful for today?

_____

_____

_____

_____

» How did I CHOOSE to be happy today?

_____

_____

_____

_____

» How did my happiness or lack of happiness affect others today?

_____

_____

_____

_____

» What more could I have done to be happy today?

_____

_____

_____

_____

Being happy doesn't mean that everything is perfect.
It means that you've decided to look beyond the imperfections.

DAY 13

DATE: _ _ _ _ _ _ _ _ _ _

Circle the appropriate answer:

Was I happy today?	Y/N
Did I eat nutritiously?	Y/N
Did I exercise today?	Y/N
Did I sleep well last night?	Y/N
Did I meditate today?	Y/N
Did I take time for myself today?	Y/N

» What am I grateful for today?

_____

_____

_____

_____

» How did I CHOOSE to be happy today?

_____

_____

_____

_____

» How did my happiness or lack of happiness affect others today?

_____

_____

_____

_____

» What more could I have done to be happy today?

_____

_____

_____

_____

The grass is greener where you water it.

DAY 14

DATE: _ _ _ _ _ _ _ _ _

Circle the appropriate answer:

Was I happy today?	Y/N
Did I eat nutritiously?	Y/N
Did I exercise today?	Y/N
Did I sleep well last night?	Y/N
Did I meditate today?	Y/N
Did I take time for myself today?	Y/N

» What am I grateful for today?

_____

_____

_____

_____

» How did I CHOOSE to be happy today?

_____

_____

_____

_____

» How did my happiness or lack of happiness affect others today?

_____

_____

_____

_____

» What more could I have done to be happy today?

_____

_____

_____

_____

Find out where joy resides, and give it a voice far beyond singing.
For to miss the joy is to miss all. - Robert Louis Stevenson

DAY 15

DATE: _ _ _ _ _ _ _ _ _ _

Circle the appropriate answer:

Was I happy today?	Y/N
Did I eat nutritiously?	Y/N
Did I exercise today?	Y/N
Did I sleep well last night?	Y/N
Did I meditate today?	Y/N
Did I take time for myself today?	Y/N

» What am I grateful for today?

_____

_____

_____

_____

» How did I CHOOSE to be happy today?

_____

_____

_____

_____

» How did my happiness or lack of happiness affect others today?

_____

_____

_____

_____

» What more could I have done to be happy today?

_____

_____

_____

_____

Nobody can take away your pain, so don't let anyone take away your happiness.

DAY 16

DATE: _ _ _ _ _ _ _ _ _ _

Circle the appropriate answer:

Was I happy today?	Y/N
Did I eat nutritiously?	Y/N
Did I exercise today?	Y/N
Did I sleep well last night?	Y/N
Did I meditate today?	Y/N
Did I take time for myself today?	Y/N

» What am I grateful for today?

_____

_____

_____

_____

» How did I CHOOSE to be happy today?

_____

_____

_____

_____

» How did my happiness or lack of happiness affect others today?

_____

_____

_____

» What more could I have done to be happy today?

_____

_____

_____

Never search your happiness in others, it will make you feel alone.
Search it in yourself and you will feel happy even when you are
left alone

DAY 17

DATE: _ _ _ _ _ _ _ _ _ _

Circle the appropriate answer:

Was I happy today?	Y/N
Did I eat nutritiously?	Y/N
Did I exercise today?	Y/N
Did I sleep well last night?	Y/N
Did I meditate today?	Y/N
Did I take time for myself today?	Y/N

» What am I grateful for today?

_____

_____

_____

_____

» How did I CHOOSE to be happy today?

_____

_____

_____

_____

» How did my happiness or lack of happiness affect others today?

_____

_____

_____

_____

» What more could I have done to be happy today?

_____

_____

_____

_____

Everyone chases after happiness not noticing that happiness is right at their heels.

DAY 18

DATE: _ _ _ _ _ _ _ _ _ _

Circle the appropriate answer:

Was I happy today?   Y/N
Did I eat nutritiously?   Y/N
Did I exercise today?   Y/N
Did I sleep well last night?   Y/N
Did I meditate today?   Y/N
Did I take time for myself today?   Y/N

» What am I grateful for today?

_____

_____

_____

_____

» How did I CHOOSE to be happy today?

_____

_____

_____

_____

» How did my happiness or lack of happiness affect others today?

_____

_____

_____

_____

» What more could I have done to be happy today?

_____

_____

_____

_____

To fall in love with yourself is the first secret to happiness.
- Robert Morely

DAY 19

DATE: _ _ _ _ _ _ _ _ _

Circle the appropriate answer:

Was I happy today?	Y/N
Did I eat nutritiously?	Y/N
Did I exercise today?	Y/N
Did I sleep well last night?	Y/N
Did I meditate today?	Y/N
Did I take time for myself today?	Y/N

» What am I grateful for today?

_____

_____

_____

_____

» How did I CHOOSE to be happy today?

_____

_____

_____

_____

» How did my happiness or lack of happiness affect others today?

_____

_____

_____

_____

» What more could I have done to be happy today?

_____

_____

_____

_____

Love is the master key that opens the gates of happiness.
- Oliver Wendell Holmes

DAY 20

DATE: _ _ _ _ _ _ _ _ _ _

Circle the appropriate answer:

Was I happy today?	Y/N
Did I eat nutritiously?	Y/N
Did I exercise today?	Y/N
Did I sleep well last night?	Y/N
Did I meditate today?	Y/N
Did I take time for myself today?	Y/N

» What am I grateful for today?

_____

_____

_____

_____

» How did I CHOOSE to be happy today?

_____

_____

_____

_____

» How did my happiness or lack of happiness affect others today?

_____

_____

_____

» What more could I have done to be happy today?

_____

_____

_____

Choose your thoughts carefully. Keep what brings you peace, release what brings you suffering. And know that happiness is just a thought away. - Nishan Panwar

DAY 21

DATE: _ _ _ _ _ _ _ _ _ _

Circle the appropriate answer:

Was I happy today?	Y/N
Did I eat nutritiously?	Y/N
Did I exercise today?	Y/N
Did I sleep well last night?	Y/N
Did I meditate today?	Y/N
Did I take time for myself today?	Y/N

» What am I grateful for today?

_____

_____

_____

_____

» How did I CHOOSE to be happy today?

_____

_____

_____

_____

» How did my happiness or lack of happiness affect others today?

_____

_____

_____

_____

» What more could I have done to be happy today?

_____

_____

_____

_____

If you want to be happy, be. - Leo Tolstoy

DAY 22

DATE: _ _ _ _ _ _ _ _ _

Circle the appropriate answer:

Was I happy today?	Y/N
Did I eat nutritiously?	Y/N
Did I exercise today?	Y/N
Did I sleep well last night?	Y/N
Did I meditate today?	Y/N
Did I take time for myself today?	Y/N

» What am I grateful for today?

_____

_____

_____

_____

» How did I CHOOSE to be happy today?

_____

_____

_____

_____

» How did my happiness or lack of happiness affect others today?

_____

_____

_____

_____

» What more could I have done to be happy today?

_____

_____

_____

_____

Happiness is a direction, not a place. - Sydney J. Harris

DAY 23

DATE: _ _ _ _ _ _ _ _ _ _

Circle the appropriate answer:

Was I happy today?	Y/N
Did I eat nutritiously?	Y/N
Did I exercise today?	Y/N
Did I sleep well last night?	Y/N
Did I meditate today?	Y/N
Did I take time for myself today?	Y/N

» What am I grateful for today?

_____

_____

_____

_____

» How did I CHOOSE to be happy today?

_____

_____

_____

_____

» How did my happiness or lack of happiness affect others today?

_____

_____

_____

_____

» What more could I have done to be happy today?

_____

_____

_____

_____

It's not happiness that brings us gratitude. It's gratitude that brings us happiness.

DAY 24

DATE: _ _ _ _ _ _ _ _ _ _

Circle the appropriate answer:

Was I happy today?	Y/N
Did I eat nutritiously?	Y/N
Did I exercise today?	Y/N
Did I sleep well last night?	Y/N
Did I meditate today?	Y/N
Did I take time for myself today?	Y/N

» What am I grateful for today?

_____

_____

_____

_____

» How did I CHOOSE to be happy today?

_____

_____

_____

_____

» How did my happiness or lack of happiness affect others today?

_____

_____

_____

_____

» What more could I have done to be happy today?

_____

_____

_____

_____

Happiness can be found even in the darkest of times if one only remembers to turn on the light. - Albus Dumbledore

DAY 25

DATE: _____

Circle the appropriate answer:

Was I happy today?   Y/N
Did I eat nutritiously?   Y/N
Did I exercise today?   Y/N
Did I sleep well last night?   Y/N
Did I meditate today?   Y/N
Did I take time for myself today?   Y/N

» What am I grateful for today?

_____

_____

_____

_____

» How did I CHOOSE to be happy today?

_____

_____

_____

_____

» How did my happiness or lack of happiness affect others today?

_____

_____

_____

_____

» What more could I have done to be happy today?

_____

_____

_____

_____

The happiness of your life depends upon the quality of your thoughts. - Marcus Aurelius

DAY 26

DATE: _ _ _ _ _ _ _ _ _

Circle the appropriate answer:

Was I happy today?	Y/N
Did I eat nutritiously?	Y/N
Did I exercise today?	Y/N
Did I sleep well last night?	Y/N
Did I meditate today?	Y/N
Did I take time for myself today?	Y/N

» What am I grateful for today?

_____

_____

_____

_____

» How did I CHOOSE to be happy today?

_____

_____

_____

_____

» How did my happiness or lack of happiness affect others today?

_____

_____

_____

_____

» What more could I have done to be happy today?

_____

_____

_____

_____

You will never be happy if you continue to search for what happiness consists of. You will never live if you are looking for the meaning of life. - Albert Einstein

DAY 27

DATE: _ _ _ _ _ _ _ _ _

Circle the appropriate answer:

Was I happy today?	Y/N
Did I eat nutritiously?	Y/N
Did I exercise today?	Y/N
Did I sleep well last night?	Y/N
Did I meditate today?	Y/N
Did I take time for myself today?	Y/N

» What am I grateful for today?

_____

_____

_____

_____

» How did I CHOOSE to be happy today?

_____

_____

_____

_____

» How did my happiness or lack of happiness affect others today?

_____

_____

_____

_____

» What more could I have done to be happy today?

_____

_____

_____

_____

Learn to let go. That is the key to happiness. - Buddha

DAY 28

DATE: _ _ _ _ _ _ _ _ _ _

Circle the appropriate answer:

Was I happy today?	Y/N
Did I eat nutritiously?	Y/N
Did I exercise today?	Y/N
Did I sleep well last night?	Y/N
Did I meditate today?	Y/N
Did I take time for myself today?	Y/N

» What am I grateful for today?

_____

_____

_____

_____

» How did I CHOOSE to be happy today?

_____

_____

_____

_____

» How did my happiness or lack of happiness affect others today?

_____

_____

_____

_____

» What more could I have done to be happy today?

_____

_____

_____

_____

*Happiness is the art of never holding in your mind the
memory of any unpleasant thing that has passed.*

DAY 29

DATE: _ _ _ _ _ _ _ _ _

Circle the appropriate answer:

Was I happy today?	Y/N
Did I eat nutritiously?	Y/N
Did I exercise today?	Y/N
Did I sleep well last night?	Y/N
Did I meditate today?	Y/N
Did I take time for myself today?	Y/N

» What am I grateful for today?

_____

_____

_____

_____

» How did I CHOOSE to be happy today?

_____

_____

_____

_____

» How did my happiness or lack of happiness affect others today?

_____

_____

_____

_____

» What more could I have done to be happy today?

_____

_____

_____

_____

When one door of happiness closes, another opens, but often we look so long at the closed door that we do not see the one that has been opened for us.-Helen Keller

DAY 30

DATE: _ _ _ _ _ _ _ _ _ _

Circle the appropriate answer:

Was I happy today?	Y/N
Did I eat nutritiously?	Y/N
Did I exercise today?	Y/N
Did I sleep well last night?	Y/N
Did I meditate today?	Y/N
Did I take time for myself today?	Y/N

» What am I grateful for today?

_____

_____

_____

_____

» How did I CHOOSE to be happy today?

_____

_____

_____

_____

» How did my happiness or lack of happiness affect others today?

_____

_____

_____

_____

» What more could I have done to be happy today?

_____

_____

_____

_____

When I look back on all these worries, I remember the story of the old man who said on his deathbed that he had had a lot of trouble in his life, most of which had never happened.-Winston Churchill

DAY 31

DATE: _ _ _ _ _ _ _ _ _

Circle the appropriate answer:

Was I happy today?	Y/N
Did I eat nutritiously?	Y/N
Did I exercise today?	Y/N
Did I sleep well last night?	Y/N
Did I meditate today?	Y/N
Did I take time for myself today?	Y/N

» What am I grateful for today?

_____

_____

_____

_____

» How did I CHOOSE to be happy today?

_____

_____

_____

_____

» How did my happiness or lack of happiness affect others today?

_____

_____

_____

_____

» What more could I have done to be happy today?

_____

_____

_____

_____

Action may not always bring happiness; but there is no happiness without action.-Benjamin Disraeli

HOW'S IT GOING?

So, it's been about a month now – I hope that you have been able to see an increase in your happiness factor. Keep it going for a cumulative effect. You can download copies of the journal pages at my website: www.gohappyyourself.com

If you would like to expand on your happiness even more, you can sign up for my 90-Day Happiness Incubator. During the 90-day program, we go deeper on all 8 petals of the Happiness Bloom, plus delve into subjects such as forgiveness, guilt and regret, envisioning the life you want, and making a solid plan to make it happen.

You can find out more about my programs at www.gohappyyourself.com

I hope you'll join us!

Jamie Lee Carmichael

ABOUT THE AUTHOR

Jamie Lee Carmichael is a Certified Professional Life Coach and author who helps people jumpstart their lives, get unstuck, find their joy again and live a happy and fruitful life...at whatever age they are.

www.GoHappyYourself.com

NOTES

_____

_____

_____

_____

_____

_____

_____

_____

_____

_____

Made in the USA
Columbia, SC
08 October 2017